LISTEN
TO ME

ALSO BY LYNN LAUBER

21 Sugar Street
White Girls

LISTEN TO ME.

WRITING LIFE

INTO MEANING

LYNN LAUBER

W · W · NORTON & COMPANY

NEW YORK LONDON

For information about permission to reproduce selections from this
book, write to Permissions, W. W. Norton & Company, Inc., 500 Fifth
Avenue, New York, NY 10110

Manufacturing by the Haddon Craftsmen, Inc.
Book design by Margaret M. Wagner
Production manager: Amanda Morrison

Library of Congress Cataloging-in-Publication Data

Lauber, Lynn.
Listen to me : writing life into meaning / Lynn Lauber.—1st ed.
p. cm.
Includes bibliographical references.
ISBN 0-393-05722-4 (hard.)
1. Authorship—Psychological aspects. 2. Authorship. I. Title.
PN171.P83L38 2003
808'.02'019—dc21

2003013975

W. W. Norton & Company, Inc., 500 Fifth Avenue, New York, N.Y. 10110
www.wwnorton.com

W. W. Norton & Company Ltd., Castle House,
75/76 Wells Street, London W1T 3QT

1 2 3 4 5 6 7 8 9 0

For two beloved Roberts
—Lauber and Kaplow—
& Barbara Wersba

Thanks to the workshop participants who over the years have shared their lives—and enriched mine—through their writing.

CONTENTS

CONTENTS

LISTEN
TO ME

INTRODUCTION

In many ways writing is the act of saying I, of imposing oneself upon other people, of saying listen to me, see it my way, change your mind.
—JOAN DIDION

Writing can be a crucial skill, like cartography. Everybody lives in the middle of a landscape. Writing can provide a map.
—PHYLLIS THEROUX

I might not have written at all if I'd had another life.

If my young parents had inched further south down Route 75 and settled in Cincinnati, or Piqua, with its all-you-can-eat cafeteria, specializing in chicken gizzards and candied yams. Or if they'd moved my sophomore year—as they'd contemplated in the incipient stages of my rebellion—to a school in the corn-fed suburbs, instead of having me fend my way in my miniskirts through the Rust Belt clamor of our small town.

If my father hadn't worked late summer evenings collecting insurance policy debits, had my mother not sat at a steel desk keypunching data so I could do what she had been unable to do—go to college and escape small-town life—my destiny would have been fractured, there'd be another version of me now: maybe the woman I saw staring out of her apartment door the last time I was home—blank-faced and ashen, any defiance long gone. Smoking a cigarette, the TV flashing in the background, a lank-haired daughter slumped on the couch.

This could have been me, perhaps *should* have been me.

Or maybe I've had this life in order to have something to write about. For without my long, heedless rebellion, my self-inflicted troubles, there wouldn't have been so much I wanted to say.

I started writing nearly thirty years ago when I was the most lost and feckless girl imaginable—a sneak, a liar, an outsider—all traits that no one ever tells you are assets for writing, even if they're trouble out in the world.

By the time I was sixteen, I'd had a child by my African-American boyfriend—a child I'd given up for adoption; I'd become alienated from the town I'd grown up in, and worn out my parents. I didn't know what would become of me.

And so I wrote . . . about odd, baleful girls from small places; about exile, the allure of other people's neighborhoods, revenge. I used clichés without knowing it and imitated anyone in my path. This was writing that went on in private and remained there, work no one wanted or read or financed. And so it has mostly remained.

I also wrote about the daughter I gave up for adoption years before I ever laid eyes on her.

It was the policy of the unwed mothers' home where I spent seven sodden, lethargic months for the mother to be put to sleep during labor so that the baby could be whisked off to adoption officials sight unseen.

This may have been a neat way of dealing with pesky issues of maternal attachment, but this act caused a great break between my heart and body; a network of fissures that transformed me into a walking bag of jutting bones and jangling parts.

I began to write then as a way of restoring my fractured self and calling up my phantom baby. In and out of college, with A's in drama and D's in German, in semidetached brick apartments with roaches on the walls, in cathedral-ceilinged efficiencies in Thurber Village (before I knew who Thurber was), on benches in bus terminals, I wrote on envelopes and the backs of pay stubs, and I imagined a girl who was cinnamon-colored, tea-toned, but mostly golden.

Alchemy, I was trying for—I who had never heard of the word.

By handling the material of my life, picking up the facts and turning them over, exaggerating and connecting them, I became involved in navigational work, even though I wasn't aware of it at the time. In this way, writing became an act of inner charting.

Who was I far down there? What was I doing with this life of mine?

Often it seemed I didn't even know what I believed until I wrote it, as if writing were the arrow that pierced a subterranean region rich with metaphor, wisdom, and foreknowledge.

As I continued to write, and attended workshops, then began leading them myself, I saw how this was not unusual but the common experience, that most people had stories they were eager to write and that it did them some deep inner good to do so. I saw that this kind of writing gave people a way of making a crucial link between their inner and outer worlds.

Karolyn Kempner writes:

> It is inherent in the nature of human beings to seek to discover and verify the meaning of life. We do not so much have to go looking for that meaning, as to let ourselves remember it, to let the meaning emerge and speak to us from the context of our lives. What is needed is an instrument and a method by which we can establish an ongoing relationship with the meaning that is already there.

> It has been my experience that personal writing can go a long way in fulfilling this function; as an instrument of self-awareness and reflection, it often serves to illuminate life.

The Power of Stories

Writing is a way of listening to ourselves, putting an ear to the wall of our interiors, discerning the rustle of our souls.

It is an act of power, and many of us aren't accustomed to power.

When I first attended writing workshops, the only way I could read my work was turned away, facing a wall. I wasn't accustomed to the sound of my own voice. *Listen to me,* I was saying, and I couldn't believe that anyone would.

The only power I knew then was from displaying my body, wearing the miniskirts I had my mother whip up on her Singer, skirts so short that if I bent over to pick up a pencil, my hind quarters were displayed as in a butcher shop.

Power was car horns and catcalls as I sashayed down local streets in my halter tops—but it was a short, flat power that left nothing in its wake except the desire to do it again, get it again.

I was well aware of my glossy exterior; I knew my emotions, which pulled me around like a renegade horse. But my mind was unknown to me, and could not be reached by the usual methods, by pop quizzes and multiple-choice questions. It was mired deep in mud, a blind fish, unaccustomed to light.

It was only through writing that I realized I was not the decorative shell I was trying so hard to impersonate.

Writing brought me down into myself.

I was joined together, reunited, through words.

This book is an account of how I have struggled to write my life into meaning, of how writing has led the way, trailing awareness in its wake. My purpose is not only to share my experience but to encourage others to explore and savor their own personal material and write about it in the deepest, truest way.

This is writing for its own sweet sake, as an illumination right in the middle of life—not a big production that requires degrees, special skills, or a ravishing ambition.

People are barred from the considerable pleasures of personal writing by the belief that they have to be specially gifted or ambitious or that their lives have to be particularly worthy.

Yet each of our lives has been filled with drama and grandeur; we all have a natural voice that's often been tamped down by hypercriticalness, English classes, callousness, lack of space and time.

Between the informality of a grocery list and the finely wrought prose of a Pulitzer Prize winner is a middle way, a fertile grove where any of us can wander.

In a time when there is little space for listening, when people who yearn to reflect are relegated to the therapist's couch, personal writing may be one of the last ways we have of keeping track of each other and ourselves.

WRITING OUT OF YOUR LIFE

Everything is held together with stories. . . . That is all that is holding us together, stories and compassion.

—BARRY LOPEZ

Pursue, keep up with, circle round and round your life. . . . Know your own bone; gnaw at it, bury it, unearth it, gnaw at it still. . . .

—HENRY DAVID THOREAU

In memory we never tire of reflecting on the same events. I spent many summers in my childhood on a farm with an uncle who told stories endlessly. This, I now see, was his method of working the raw material of his life, his way of turning his experience round and round in the rotation that stories provide. Out of that incessant storytelling I knew he found added depths of meaning. Storytelling is an excellent way of caring for the soul. It helps us see the themes that circle in our lives, the deep themes that tell the myths that we live.

—THOMAS MOORE

When I was a girl, my father had more stories to tell than my mother, but they seemed to make her nervous. There was something about his reminiscences that made her come into the room and dish up a task—any task—to distract or waylay him.

Even as a child I knew why she did this. The stories of my father's pinched childhood, the privations of his beloved, neglected mother, wandered too near a dark lake of feeling where my mother seemed chary of letting us go.

Like the stone quarry on the edge of town where high school girls disappeared forever, leaving behind only their heartbreaking vinyl shoes, these were bottomless pits from which we might never emerge.

And storytelling seemed excessive then, in the late fifties and early sixties—self-involved and out of sync with the forward march of our newly plastic world. Who wanted to dangle their feet in the murky thirties or forties? Who cared about the past?

Still, I registered the scraps my father got out when my mother was elsewhere; I gleaned enough to glimpse the sorrow and the pity that often underlay the brisk surface life we were supposed to be trying to live.

But it was my mother's stories, the real facts about the vexations and malfunctions of the female heart and body that I really wanted to hear—one egg bearer to the next.

I know now that being a rebellious girl from a small town is one of the oldest stories in the world. In fact, it was also my mother's story. But by the time I was an adolescent, my mother was a respectable wife and mother and did not harp on her discontents and displacements to the likes of me.

So all I usually heard were narratives straight from the Bible—how the Reisinger married the Dieffeldorf and then mothered the Billy before disappearing into the ether of the Midwest.

I listened to some of these sagas while watching my grandmother sew wedding gowns in her hot back room, a warren of seed pearls and tulle. Trains were her specialty, following in the wake of brides, a flood of silk.

My mother had once stood in her own homemade puddle, her lips dark as chocolate, as if a swirled dessert. I knew girls were supposed to manage this once at the beginning of their lives—to stand inert, a burning offering. And since this was the one theme running through every female story I heard, it was also the thing I didn't want to do.

Part of my later rebellion may have been only this, that

I wanted to start another story cycle, to branch off the well-lit path and see what a girl could get into besides a wedding gown, even if it was only trouble.

The fact is that stories matter deeply to us; we yearn both to hear and to tell them.

We are tuned, as if exquisite instruments, for beginnings, middles, and endings.

Five Reasons to Write out of Your Life

1.   TO LEAVE YOUR MARK

Writing is a way of saying: *Here I am. This is what it feels like to be me, in this place, in this part of the century.*

It can be a testimony against obliteration.

In the family tree on my father's side, the women seem only to have been born, married, and died. You might find bits of them elsewhere, stitched in a quilt or tucked in a recipe, but otherwise they've vanished—only their maiden names and middle initials, their entrance and departure dates survive.

Not that the men fared much better, but they at least trailed their jobs behind them—tailor or oil rigger or shoe soler—even if their accompanying tales were lost.

So why does this matter?

Because each generation has to figure out all over again what it means to be human, a Smith, a woman.

Writing out of your life is a fine method of bequeathment, a way of handing down what you've lived and known, of reaching out a hand in kinship across time.

Recently when I talked to my mother, she passed along two images from her childhood that I'd never known before.

One was that there was a lilac bush outside her bedroom window, a lavender cloud that filled with yellow canaries each summer.

Another was how she stood at the bottom of a staircase, listening to my grandmother's "Oh!" of pain traveling out of a bedroom where she was laboring to deliver my uncle, until my grandfather solemnly led her away, now displaced from her revered only-child position, as I later was by my brother.

Wild canaries in the midst of northwestern Ohio! My stoic grandmother's vocal, personal pain!

My mother was in her seventies and I almost fifty when she passed along this little plate of tantalizing facts, making me marvel at the great otherness of even those we love.

I have a friend who encouraged her mother to write down scenes of her life as an antidote to depression and isolation. In the process of typing up these reminiscences she was amazed by her mother's private woes and struggles, many of which she'd never heard about before.

These writings made her aware of her mother as a complex, separate character pre-motherhood, pre-*her*—and of herself as a late arrival, a mere second-act plot point in the tale of her mother's life.

It is chastening and valuable to see ourselves in the stories of others, as secondary, even minor characters. To view our mothers as charmers, our fathers as agents of sexual desire, our grandparents as rabble-rousers and rebels.

Death is often the sad reminder of all the questions never asked, the tales lost for good.

E. M. Forster says:

The present flowed by them like a stream. The tree rustled. It had made music before they were born, and would continue after their deaths, but its song was of the moment.

2. FOR SELF-REVELATION AND AWARENESS

If you want to write, there's something you want to say, and it's good for you to say it.

People write to make sense of their lives, to figure out what they think and feel, to verify who they are.

My grandmother used to tell a story about her first day as the manageress of an expanded school cafeteria system, when by some vast miscalculation three hundred children showed up for school lunch instead of the sixty she'd expected.

She found herself with a herd of hungry children at the cafeteria door and only enough Johnny Marzetti and Ambrosia Surprise to feed a fifth of them.

Then came the triumphant part of her story, the part she loved to tell: how she pulled open door after door of the pantry, searching for what she could serve; how she took government surplus cans of boned chicken and turned them into sandwiches, mixed green beans and corn to make succotash.

She told her mutinous cooks, testy former wives now tough and estrogenless, to boil vast pans of water. If nothing else, she could serve perfection salad, an Ohio specialty, pale lime Jell-O with chopped cabbage and celery.

In the end, her ingenuity prevailed. I, her prime listener, never doubted it, having been fattened early at her groaning table. But I still loved how this tale harkened back to the biblical story of Jesus and the multiplied loaves, one of the few Bible stories I retained from Sunday school. And how it validated the way she, a midwestern woman who wasn't even supposed to work, had one day combined all her native talents—for emergency management and cool-headedness under pressure—and scraped up enough to make do, just as she did for the hoboes, hungry from the railroad yard, who knocked on her back door some nights.

This story verified something I'd known since I was a girl—that with my grandmother, you would never go hungry.

Storytelling seems to be a remedy for so much that ails us. In one of my workshops, a quiet, self-effacing woman lit up like an incandescent bulb whenever she read her work.

And what was she writing about? Feelings of loss over the death of a child, her memories of childhood, her daily trials—in other words, the same pathos and heartache that flows through any ordinary life.

She had been coming to the workshop for several months when she suddenly disappeared.

"What happened to Rose?" I asked one of the students who was her friend.

The woman studied me, then said, "She died."

Seeing my shock, she went on, "She didn't want you to know she was sick. She didn't want to be treated any differently."

For a moment my mind scrambled about: Had I been attentive to her, had I praised her efforts enough? How could I have sat there for so many weeks, oblivious to her struggles?

As if reading my mind, the woman said, "She got so much pleasure from what she wrote."

And then I remembered the wash of pink rising up Rose's neck and infusing her face as she read, and I thought, *Even then.*

3. FOR COMPANIONSHIP AND CONNECTION

Lauren Slater says:

> The ability to use words, to tell a story, is so central to having human relationships, that the lack of it is one of the central features of schizophrenia. In that case, the loss of language cuts off the schizophrenic not only from deep sources of self, but also from connections with others. What we all want our stories, however meager, to do is break the barrier of isolation and thrust us into a feeling of community, even if we don't see the faces of those who read us.

There is no denying the power of stories to inspire, sustain, guide, console, soothe, and comfort. Writing provides companionship and access to the larger human community. Words link us and remind us that we're not alone. When you read my words or I read yours, we are bound together. James Baldwin said, "You think your pain and heartbreak is unprecedented in all the world and then you read."

A stranger sitting beside me on a recent flight interrupted my reading to tell me, apropos of nothing, how his buddy saved his life one night in Korea forty years ago: "We were sleeping in foxholes in the mountains; it was twenty below zero. They sent out scouts in the morning to make trails for the rest of us to follow. We got up and began following them, but I fell off the trail into a ravine and was covered in snow. My friend turned around and couldn't find me, but he saw my rifle butt sticking out of the snow. He got a length of chain and pulled me out. Later he told me, 'I should have just left you there, you were such a pain in the ass!' "

Then he looked me in the eyes and laughed.

This account had the cadence of a well-worn tale. So why did this stranger need to tell it again to me? Because something deep in us needs to tell each other stories—and to be listened to in return.

In writing workshops, people who arrive looking pinched and tense depart looking eased and freshened, as if an eraser had been passed over their faces. People who come in with chips on their shoulders and doubt on their faces are softened by writing's greatest reminder: that, as Wendell Barry says, what we have in common is greater than what sets us apart.

There's a theory in physics, Bell's theorem, that says that two particles once connected are never separated, that they are stuck together by "space entanglement." Although we can't see this, we can feel it. And whenever we listen to someone's story or read their words, a filament of connection is forged.

4. TO BE A WITNESS

Writing out of your life is a form of testifying, of being a witness to your place and time.

Here the Russian poet Anna Akhmatova speaks of the years 1937–1938, when her husband and son were sent to prison camps and she waited with hundreds of other women in the cold for news that never came.

In the terrible years of the Yezhov terror I spent seventeen months waiting in line outside the prison in Leningrad. One day somebody in the crowd identified me. Standing behind me was a woman, with lips blue from the cold, who had, of course, never heard me called by name before. Now she started out of the torpor common to us all and asked me in a whisper (everyone whispered there): "Can you describe this?"

And I said: "I can."

Then something like a smile passed fleetingly over what had once been her face.

The Need to Say It

The first writing workshop I ever led was for a group of elderly East European refugees who arrived clutching their purses in clouds of Emeraude and Prince Matchiabelli. They'd been hoping for an hour of bingo and were none too pleased when they found I was there to encourage them to write about their lives.

"Who wants to hear about our lives?" they said. "What do we have to say?"

"Just give it a try," I said, passing out paper. "Start with: 'My mother told me,' then write the first thing that comes into your head and keep going."

In response, one woman blew her nose; another laboriously unwrapped a mint. Several others regarded me mutinously, as if they were weighing whether it was worth the effort to hoist themselves up and leave.

Then finally, one by one, they lowered their heads to their pages, and there was silence except for the chicken scratch of graphite against paper.

I walked out into the hall, then looked back in at their moving hands. I couldn't believe how exhilarated I felt.

Right underneath the skin of so many of us are stories just waiting to be told. After my college English professor wrote me a note encouraging my writing, I placed the slip of paper in my wallet with my driver's license and Social Security card and other validations of identity. The notion that what I had to say might be worthy was as astounding a proposition as I had ever heard. Some essential component in me had been noticed, and my former life as a one-dimensional creature trapped in a mirror began a slow, sure shattering.

This was in the 1970s, when the world was full of girls like me, wandering across campus in peasant dresses, bra-less, without a fact to our names.

No one knew either my past or present; even disrobed, padding through shabby student apartments, no one noticed the gory hole in my chest.

But when I didn't know what to do with myself, when I was so sad that all I could do was lie in bed, it wasn't a man or pill that saved me, but making symbols on paper, an odd act of meditation for a girl like me.

By putting words on paper I relocated the creature I'd

left in childhood, the chapped-lipped, self-satisfied girl who still held the golden globe of her unassailable self.

When I returned to the room at the senior center, the class was still at it. By now they'd been writing for nearly an hour, glaucoma, arthritis, and all.

"Does anyone want to read what they've written?" I asked, and before I could even finish, their hands shot up.

The real bingo lady was left cooling her heels in the hallway that day while each of the reluctant old women raised herself up on a cane or leaned on a walker and read stories that made sweat run down the small of my back.

Tales of exile and Bavarian childhoods; hiking in the Alps, dying in the camps. One woman with purple digits on her inner arm opened her mouth like a cat and wailed. The room smelled hot by the time they had finished, as if an electrical wire had shorted out.

Since then I've continued to witness the power and poetry of personal writing that takes place far from the eye of the publishing world—how the unbridled self often displays itself like a rare bird in stuffy library rooms and high school cafeterias. How the truth unfurls, gorgeous in its plainness, and the pattern of a life can be discerned like a fossilized leaf in shale.

I've watched grown men from the highway department weep at the memory of their mothers; waitresses cover their faces as they describe the girls they once were. I've seen people forge connections, encounter lost truths, and stanch old wounds.

The purpose of this work is not to be good or clever or worthy, but to allow you to express what's true.

Alice

One of the participants of my first workshop wrote:

My favorite darling when I was young was my grand-mother in the Palatinat of the Rhine. My good parents went in the summertime to resorts like Switzerland, Marienbad, and Karlsbad. My sister and I were put on the train in Munich; so as not to forget, our toothbrushes were around our necks. Grandma or her daughter Natalie waited at the station to bring us to her cozy home in a lit-tle village. Vineyards beautified the place, a wonderful synagogue and two churches. We children from the big city of Munich visited the neighbors—they had big vineyards and a carriage with two horses, and they often took us on rides. Our special interest was the Reverend with his family and their big garden with delicious berries, apples, and cherries. We also visited our favorite cows; they gave us milk by hand, and we found the swallow nests we loved so much. And Grandmother baked the most delicious cakes every week, six to eight kinds, and my sister and I always gained eight pounds, but in this time we did not care.

This was Alice, born in Munich, an early suffragette whose dental surgeon husband had stuck his head in their gas oven at the rise of Hitler, whose only son had survived the child transport only to die in a domestic plane crash. Alice, battered yet buoyant, who had brought across the Atlantic remnants of a vanished world—threadbare tapestries, porcelain hounds, and sepia photos of herself drinking schnapps in Alpine resorts.

At ninety-two, she picked her way into class on a red cane plastered with address labels, the fabric of her face scored and pleated, then hitched to the right, the result of the severing of an ischius facial nerve during labor. (But why had her face been cut during labor? I always wondered.)

I couldn't believe her: the way she hung out the car window at the George Washington Bridge and called out to the tollkeeper, "I want your job!"; how she was fascinated by scenery off the Cross Bronx Expressway; how after a potato truck rear-ended us when we'd driven to Long Island, I found her propped on her cane, charming a circle of policemen, exclaiming, "I've never been in an accident before!"

How even when she wept, speaking conversational German at her son's graveside, she did so without self-pity and was always threatening to brighten and bite into the next new thing.

It was probably crazy to fall in love with a ninety-two-year-old woman, but I couldn't help it. And when she died, far too soon, I looked down into the hole in the world she left.

How could I keep her, I who couldn't draw, who wasn't articulate enough even to describe her out loud?

But given a piece of paper, I could go off in a corner and try.

And because you've just read this, she's now alive in you, too. Alice Benario, née Politzer, 1892–1988.

5. TO HOLD ON TO SOMEONE . . .

This is the fifth, perhaps best reason of all to write out of your life.

Consider your life path—where you came from and where you're going.

Has your life been easy, hard, something in between?

What has fulfilled you most on your journey?

What do you look forward to now?

Set a timer and write a fifteen-minute outer autobiography, beginning with the phrase "I was born." Write swiftly and without planning.

Reset the timer for another fifteen minutes. Take a second sheet and write your inner autobiography, beginning with the phrase "I feel."

CHAPTER 2

WRITING OUT OF REVENGE

Write hard and clear about what hurts.

—ERNEST HEMINGWAY

Writing, I think, is not apart from living. Writing is a kind of double living. The writer experiences everything twice. Once in reality and once in that mirror which waits always before or behind.

—CATHERINE BOWEN

One day when I was sunk deep in a scene set in my hometown and starring a character I'd cobbled together using a smile belonging to this one and a foot belonging to that, the phone rang and there was the prototype—the real man still in the real town, which I had also altered and miniaturized, like a town under a snow dome. Except I hadn't idealized it, I had done the opposite—shrunken and vilified it until it was the way it seemed when I was a girl, dead-hearted and static, with its dusty appliance shops and prostitutes walking through the rubbly downtown; the county museum with its display of swallowed objects, extracted from the bronchial trees of local residents: hairpins, buttons, and tarnished dimes.

This town had been the backwater of my youth, my jinxer and thwarter, the original seat of my discontent, the place I wrote about in revenge for its being too small for me, for not offering the space, the spice, I yearned for.

It was only after I left that I saw that the real town couldn't have been *that* bad, and I tried to verify its true character whenever I returned. But no matter how many malls or renovations reshaped the landscape, I could only experience it in the twisted way of my youth, less as a place than as a suffocating personage, who loathed me but also didn't want to let me go, who would have been happy to lure me back to a couch with cigarettes and daytime talk shows.

And so I stepped back within its boundaries, gingerly, with some feeling of threat, as if I might be mired there again forever, or apprehended for having so reviled it.

But the truth was that the town never registered my visits. Even though I felt I should stand out in all my exile and diffidence, that it should somehow show on me that I had been to another Athens besides the one in southern Ohio, the sad truth was that it didn't—I appeared in no way different from anyone else.

I did not shine in a special light. I was just another middle-aged daughter with her mother, trolling through shoes at the bargain outlet.

Revenge is a good, strong motivating reason to write— and it can be directed against anything—a place, a lover—even silence.

The only time I'm liberated from the tongue-tied mincer I've been most of my life is when I write. Then I become surer, wiser, bolder, a figure who knows what she means and isn't cowed to say it.

Francine du Plessix Gray writes:

I write out of a desire for revenge against reality, to destroy forever the stuttering powerless child I once was,

39

to gain the love and attention that silenced child never had, to allay the disappointment I still have with myself; to be something other than what I am.

Some of my most productive workshops have been populated with older women who have spent a lifetime in relative silence, sitting on their hands, clamping shut their mouths.

To observe them opening up is to experience the roaring unleashing of years of held-back rage and truth. For women who have grown up silent and subservient, letting it all rip in writing, saying what previously seemed unspeakable, can be especially liberating.

Carolyn Heilbrun writes: "above all other prohibitions, what has been forbidden to women is anger, together with the open admission of the desire for power and control over one's life. . . ."

Men may not have difficulty with silence, but they have their own problems in displaying emotion. In personal writing workshops they often resemble rumbling volcanoes, spitting traces of smoke until they finally erupt, railing over the abandonment of a father, the death of a brother or a mother who didn't give them enough love.

Such writing can help deliver us from an experience that haunts us; it can lance a long-festering boil. Frank McCourt says, of writing about his impoverished childhood in *Angela's Ashes:* "All along I wanted to do this badly. I would have to do it or I would have died howling."

When Dylan Thomas wrote: "Do not go gentle into that good night. / Rage, rage against the dying of the light," he was railing against the end of his father's life and, indirectly, the inevitable end of his own. He was raging at his loss and memorializing it, lifting it up and weaving it into art. This kind of writing has a dual purpose—it helps the writer deal with the trauma of loss as well as soothes those who read it, who have been through the same grief.

Poet Jill Bialosky writes:

If you've ever seen Eric Fischl's painting "What Stands Between the Artist" or Frida Kahlo's "The Broken Column," there is no mistaking the assertion that art is born from some kind of human torment or suffering. It is the back story to any valued poem or story, though not necessarily the center or the subject matter. It is what fuels the artist to put pen to paper. Writing is a way of seeing the world, regaining meaning from experience. A friend of mine, another writer, once said that writing is an act of revenge, born out of anger. I initially resisted the sentiment. As a writer, I did not want to believe that my work was driven by anger. I chose to see it as driven by necessity and desire. But when I considered the notion further it occurred to me that what we were arguing was a matter of semantics. I preferred to see the act of writing as a means of recording some human truth, of presenting a notion of reality, an undercurrent, and dramatizing it. But the desire to seek truth through art is born out of the idea that a truth needs to be uncovered, and fueling that desire is a yearning for redemption. Perhaps anger is part of that yearning, and that muted over the course of the transcendence of experience into art, is what gives a work its sense of urgency.

Rage as Fuel

Rage, anger, revenge can all fuel writing, making tangible what has been amorphous and free-floating. This writing can be purgative, even when you share it with no one else.

I once wrote a long grousing essay about a bullying woman I was having a difficult time ghostwriting for. It was a pleasure to write down all the things I couldn't stand about her but couldn't afford to say out loud; to expose her combination of ignorance and haughtiness, the way she dropped names and mispronounced words.

Simply talking about her didn't work; only when I wrote

was I able to release the catalogue of complaints and slights that had piled up in the back of my throat.

I took a long, savoring time writing it, right down to fantasy scenes where I held forth with cutting dialogue and had the satisfying last word.

I wrote: "It's a withering experience, trying to be perky, streetwise, lighthearted on someone else's behalf. What if you don't feel perky? What if you secretly find your subject vapid, corny, or, worse, loathsome? How opaque and robotic and voiceless can you be expected to sound?"

When I finished, I considered trying to publish this piece. But in the end I didn't; it wasn't the point or worth the trouble. The act of writing had drained the venom and cleared my mind of at least some of the poisonous feelings. It wasn't that they had vanished, but they didn't dominate me any longer.

Writing can do that.

Joyce Maynard used such fuel to write about her love affair as a young woman with J. D. Salinger, a relationship that she was meant to remain silent about, given Salinger's great antipathy toward publicity of any kind. *At Home in the World* was a cautionary tale about the risks of a young girl's voice being overcome by a famous author. By refusing to protect Salinger's privacy and laying bare her suffering, she exacted a kind of revenge.

Writing unsent letters to people who have hurt or betrayed us is another way of clearing the air, discharging emotions that have been pent up and gone unexpressed. The letter is a form that encourages a sense of immediacy and the feeling that you are speaking directly to someone. Being aware that the letter will never be sent allows you to be candid and free.

You can also write letters to those you have lost through death but still have unfinished business with, even to versions of yourself—for example, to yourself as a girl or older woman. While we all wish to be heard and understood by others, these kinds of letters are for your sake alone. Exposing your anger to the light and letting it breathe can help you release and finally let it go.

Lynda Van Devanter, a nurse who entered the Vietnam War an idealist and exited it a year later bitter and disheartened, initially buried the pain of the horrors she witnessed, then chronicled them in a memoir *Home Before Morning*. Devanter said that she had first tried "to exorcise the Vietnam War from my mind and heart," but through writing had ended up illustrating "that the war doesn't have to own me, I can own it."

Write a letter that you have no intention of sending to someone—living or dead—who has hurt or betrayed you, someone to whom you have previously been unable to express your feelings.

Start writing with the phrase "I always wanted to tell you," then spill out your resentments and grievances. Release the rage; say all you didn't say before. Rant and rave and curse. Continue with whatever occurs to you, without censoring until you have run out of words.

You can also write in this way to a part of yourself you feel betrayed or victimized by, such as the self you abused by drinking heavily or taking drugs or the self who committed a shameful act.

WRITING TO HEAL

Give sorrow words.

—SHAKESPEARE

Writing is a form of therapy; sometimes I wonder how all those who do not write, compose or paint can manage to escape the madness, the melancholia, the panic fear which is inherent in the human situation.

—GRAHAM GREENE

There is something in the very nature of writing about our deepest thoughts and feelings that is healing and cathartic. Turning pain and sorrow into narrative often has a transformative power. There is a potency to the act of writing words that sets it apart from simply speaking them, a process that seems to take place between the brain and the pen. This mind-body connection is one often felt by students, who report feeling markedly better after a writing session or class where they've written about their deep emotions.

When we're faced with overwhelming loss or trauma, our thoughts become split and fragmented. The experiences are so difficult to integrate that we often keep the broken shards trapped within us, sharp and untouchable. But writing is a way of translating these experiences into a coherent narrative that can allow them to be processed.

In wondering about the ability of Justice Thurgood Marshall to confront racism and hatred and remain intact, Sandra Day O'Connor writes that part of the answer lay in his capacity for narration. "His stories reflected a truly expansive personality—the perspective of a man who immersed himself in human suffering and then translated that suffering in a way that others could bear and understand."

D. H. Lawrence wrote: "One sheds one's sicknesses in books—repeats and presents again one's emotions to be master of them."

You don't have to actually write a book for this to happen. Writing regularly and freely about one's thoughts and feelings can be therapeutic, as one of my workshop participants, Fran Smith, who survived years of childhood incest, attests:

> I can say with absolute certainty that writing helps me. . . .
>
> Until I get something down on paper, something real, not only about the facts but the feelings, something in my mind keeps trying to hide the truth . . . to hide who I really am. It's like trying to eat an octopus—the octopus objects, clouds the water, and either tangles around me or slips away under a rock where I can't find it. It's like I see things through a fog. I pretend to myself that I'm over it, but inside I'm getting all twisted up in tentacles. . . . I have to pin the octopus down, carve him up, and digest him bit by bit. . . .

There is a long tradition of writing as a way to transcend grief and loss, to repair the self and memorialize pain.

William Styron explored his long bout of depression in *Darkness Visible*. In her diaries, Virginia Woolf faced down the demons that plagued her life as a writer. In Maya

Angelou's *I Know Why the Caged Bird Sings*, the author confronted the suffering of her childhood and early life.

In *Man's Search for Meaning*, psychiatrist Viktor Frankl recounted the horrors of his years in Nazi concentration camps, where he lost all his family except for his sister. When all the familiar goals in life are taken away, what remains, according to Frankl, is the ability to "choose one's attitude in a given set of circumstances." Frankl concluded that the real thrust of human life is to discover its meaning and purpose.

Writing can help with these discoveries.

Knowing none of this, I wrote over and over about the pain I'd experienced as a young woman—giving up a child, wounding myself and my family—in what I now see was some blind instinct to try and scorch it from my soul.

Five Ways Writing Can Heal You

IT CAN:

1. PROVIDE CATHARSIS

A death is still a death, an illness still an illness, but writing about it can provide a certain catharsis, a way of putting it in its place. By allowing emotional release, writing can help us handle the anguish of bereavement and loss.

Susan Zimmerman says: "The act of writing provides structure and order to the chaos of grief. It taps into the healing power of your own unconscious. By giving voice to fears, anger and despair, by letting go of old dreams and hopes, our self-healing powers come into play."

2. RINSE PAIN

Writing about pain doesn't banish it, but it can soothe it, "rinse" it, as one student put it. The very act of writing can bring about an inner focus that redirects energy and drains away the acute painfulness that can dominate consciousness. Deep writing can pull you away from your troubles and concentrate your energies in a creative flow.

3. BRING YOURSELF TOGETHER

Writing about your life can be an integrative process, where the girl you once were runs smack into the woman you've become, and they find a way to share what they know. Writing can illuminate themes and patterns in your life; it can sharpen your future focus. Through writing, you may discover that self-deception or victimhood has been a recurring theme in your life. Seeing this can help you change direction and take new paths.

4. NAVIGATE YOUR DEEP SELF

Writing can pull you down into the unconscious, a place you rarely have the time or means to visit. Writing about your feelings, impulses, and inner secrets can give you access to reservoirs of strength and inner wisdom. Exploring these depths can help you keep track of yourself.

5. PROVIDE PERSPECTIVE

Writing about yourself and those in your life can help you view a situation—and yourself—in a new, clearer way. Turning the people in your life into characters, writing from their point of view, viewing yourself in the third person—all these devices are ways of allowing you to "see" again. Suddenly your lover may be imbued with qualities you were unable to see before; your mother's life may not seem so tragic; your sister's treachery may be easier to understand.

Coping Through Writing

My friend Margaret started writing the story of her life in her eighties, just as she began losing her vision to macular degeneration. As her outer vision dimmed, she turned inward as a way of coping with her vanishing sight. This writing gave her life a purposeful focus during a period when her world was shrinking and darkening. Whenever I visited her I began seeing enigmatic scraps of paper saying things like *Pain 1913*.

In midlife she had worked saving houses in the Hudson River Valley, often just before they were demolished. This is what she wrote about: the bricks she repointed, the lean-tos she salvaged, the ruined porches and sagging foundations she jacked up. In particular she wrote about a brick house she saved during an especially tough time in her life.

Here, writing about stairs she sanded in this house, she ruminates on a lifetime of stairs:

> I remembered the magnificent stairs at Wells Cathedral in England, the worn and winding ascent in stone that was a glorious Te Deum in itself.
>
> And that delicious staircase in the dockside restaurant in Honfleur that led in a short flight to a bedchamber. How I remember that room! The mouthwatering smell of fine cooking rising from below, and through the blowing window curtains, the sparkle and sounds of the Honfleur waterfront.

If scraping and sanding were drudgery, the dreams and memories that flowed were sweet and diverting.

I remembered the steps my mother built, steps that led down a sandy slope to the workroom in our cottage on Lake Michigan, built by her of four-foot logs held in place by stout stakes which she drove in with a hatchet. In back of the log was the sand of the dune, which made a comfortable tread. The steps were a very creditable piece of work, and they remained for years after her death.

However, when it came time to sand, starting with my lovely Black & Decker finishing sander, I returned to the present. And how beautiful my steps were, with their shining knots and velvety, worn-down treads.

Margaret claimed this writing was "an anchor of sanity" that helped her through the transition from lightness to darkness.

Writing for Health

The process of looking back on a life and putting it on paper can provide a reflective catharsis, a sense of the integrity and meaning of existence. There is even a name for this kind of work, done late in life—reminiscence therapy.

This is what the East European women in my first workshop were involved in, though they didn't know it at the time—and neither did I.

This kind of writing can help people handle stress, deal with painful experience, and increase self-awareness.

You don't have to be eighty to find this helpful. By the time you're thirty, your life already has a shape and a theme that can be observed and reflected upon.

Such writing can also help deliver you from an experience that haunts you; it can illuminate a mystery or drain a painful memory. Studies now show that it can even be physically therapeutic.

In a British study on the health benefits of writing poetry, participants said that writing helped them reduce anxiety, cope with the pain of bereavement, and, in some cases, allowed them to stop taking medicines for depression.

Other studies have illustrated how writing about traumatic experiences can improve the immunity of healthy adults. One performed at North Dakota State University and reported in the *Journal of the American Medical Association* found that people with rheumatoid arthritis or asthma who wrote about an emotional experience or the stress in their lives, as opposed to emotionally neutral topics, found their symptoms reduced. It's not clear how this occurs, but writing about an upsetting event may interrupt the release of stress hormones that cause anxiety symptoms and can harm the immune system. A single writing exercise eased symptoms for several months.

Nicki Jacowska, author of *Write for Life*, believes that writing is an antidote to modern-day efficiency. "Large areas of human nature are being sacrificed in the race to doing things in the shortest possible time. Creative writing, on the other hand, is about unravelling and letting go."

One workshop participant told me how her father, a car salesman, had taken time out of his hectic schedule every day for forty years to write about his troubles in a series of diaries. No one knew this until they found them after his death. And there were his daily preoccupations and worries, his lost quotas, his health and financial fears, his sorrows over the deaths in his family. He had kept much of this heartache from his family, but, importantly, he had not kept it from himself.

This is a lovely example of how writing can be a solace—carving out of a living life time for self-reflection and repair.

Dr. Lisa Sanders, a Connecticut internist, was devastated when her sister, aged forty-two, died abruptly for no apparent reason. In order to handle her grief, Dr. Sanders tried to come up with a story of how this could have occurred. She assembled a differential diagnosis, consulted her sister's doctors and friends, and talked to the coroner's office. Eventually she came up with a scenario that seemed plausible—her sister, a binge drinker, had low blood potassium, which had affected her electrolytes and could have caused her heart to suddenly stop. Although this couldn't be verified by the autopsy, this scenario offered her some comfort. She says, "Ultimately science doesn't bring certainty, but it can help tell the final story in a life. After the body is buried, and medicine has finished doing all that it can, stories are what we want and really, all that we have."

Arrange two pieces of paper side by side.

Choose one of the most emotional, traumatic, or stressful experiences in your life.

On the left-hand page, write about the incident exactly as it happened.

Locate the hour, where you were, who was with you.

What did you hear and see and smell?

Use any form that is comfortable. You can write it as a straight narrative, a letter to someone, even a poem.

On the right-hand page, note any physical feelings or responses that occur while you write this account ("my heart is racing; I feel sick to my stomach") or any response that you remember from the incident ("I saw stars; I felt a pain in my side").

When you're finished, reread the results.

Does airing these emotions or feelings ease them or help you put them in perspective?

Can you note any difference in how you feel after writing?

CHAPTER 4

THE MAGIC OF AUTOMATIC WRITING

How do I know what I think until I see what I say?
— W. H. AUDEN

It still comes as a shock to realize that I don't write about what I know, but in order to find out what I know.
— PATRICIA HAMPL

If the writer isn't surprised, the reader won't be.
— FLANNERY O'CONNOR

Below the surface stream, shallow and light,
Of what we say and feel—below the stream,
As light, of what we think we feel—there flows
With noiseless current, strong, obscure and deep,
The central stream of what we feel indeed.
— MATTHEW ARNOLD

After spending my early years stomping around in high heels in revolt against what I saw as my placid, predictable background, I'm now grateful that I come from practical, hardworking people who mow their own lawns and pay for their gravestones years before they die.

My sturdy, milk-fed childhood was overseen by reliable parents who spent their days earning and saving, who had little time to read, let alone write, novels or satires.

This was in opposition to acquaintances I met once I moved to New York, whose mothers not only knew who Boccaccio was but how to spell him, whose fathers were in the midst of writing post-constructionist theory in competition with their own.

This kind of background can be as much a burden as an asset, a load of Samsonite strapped on your back. It can make it impossible to write a single sentence without falling upon it with judgments, comparisons, and the sure knowledge—certainly better not to dwell on—that there's nothing new under the sun.

Using the Unconscious

Writing stems from feeling, not intellect. The pivot upon which deep writing turns is to let the unconscious do the work; to write the words and find out what they mean later; to plunge into chaos so that the material can appear.

The best method of circumventing years of outlines, topic sentences, and comparative literature is automatic writing. It's the finest way to capture thoughts you never realized you had.

Automatic writing also helps banish the linear model that shuts down so much creative thought. It is a way to initiate regular sessions of exploratory writing, where you set off in comfortable shoes, but with no particular destination, and allow yourself to wander off the path and make new discoveries.

With automatic writing, you bypass the head and ego and write straight from the heart. This kind of writing can throw open the window to wild unvisited places, full of images and stories that have long been hidden.

One woman in a workshop harbored only the most bitter feelings for a father who had deserted her family when she was little. She toted these resentments in a knapsack; they infused every piece she wrote. But she barged into other, fonder memories when she freewrote about him, recalling facts other than his departure—a felt hat he used to wear, his chuckle, snatches of unremembered tenderness. Her face looked different after she wrote these pieces; she had come upon a soothing truth.

Through automatic writing, another woman ran into the realization that the real reason she had married her charming cad of a husband wasn't because he was her soul mate, but simply because she had wanted to have children of the same hue and cut as he was. She was seventy when she wrote—and recognized—this. After years of defending her choice of a husband, she was relieved and delighted to realize this plain truth.

This often happens with automatic writing—a realization is made, a chunk of memory dislodged, a connection snapped into place.

By following the circuitous but wise route of automatic writing, you can often approach topics that have been difficult to write about using more conscious methods.

Here Elizabeth McKenzie, a workshop participant, is able to reflect on the painful death of a friend by allowing her unconscious to connect with parallels in the natural world:

It has been almost a year since I got that news, since I lay on my bed all day crying, holding Jim's picture, sad and pissed off at the same time, how could you leave me? Late in the afternoon, I drove out to Silver Bay, walked the gravel road to a group of flat gray rocks. I sat in the sun watching the king salmon hurling their silver bodies up, dashing into the air, seemingly just for the joy of it, just because they could. Perhaps flinging themselves into the foreign matter of air is to the chinook like swimming is to me—gliding through the alternate universe, experiencing the body in the completely opposite medium. Perhaps to a fish, especially one who is momentarily airborne, her body feels suddenly light and free and boundless as mine does when I fin over the blue water, my own version of flying. The water ruffles over my skin as the air ruffles the chinook's gills—a completely foreign feeling, dangerous yet delicious. . . .

I wonder if death could be like that—like the chinook flying in the air and sun. Perhaps if we are reborn again into this world as the Buddhists believe, our time away from this life is but a chinook's moment in air—the lightness and joy of flight, the warm sun, the water sparkling below, the being wholly and completely thrusting upwards, tasting exhilaration, the gills moving over the air, the air opening each cell, a cleansing, a renewal, a reunion with the other. And the reentry—to know again the thrill of the body, the unbearable joy of being.

With automatic writing, it's possible to turn off the big red switch of your critical mind, to shut down the hectoring ego, to let loose your unbridled self—the you of you under your skin, under the covers.

The words that come to your mind using this method are often powerful and revealing.

It was through automatic writing that I came to realize that

for all my early discontent, I'd had a splendid childhood, in the brick-streeted towns of my relatives, along shipping canals, now dark, odorous backyard lanes.

Replete on my mother's side with double sets of doting elders for whom my simple existence was cause for celebration.

There were peonies in the side yards and cool walnut interiors and yellow kitchens where broad-beamed aunts handed out cut glasses of tap water, laced with iron.

I had been petted, fed rich jarred concoctions; raised high and bonneted as a flowering branch.

Perhaps only someone like me, with so much behind her, could so heedlessly rebel.

I had not quite registered that I believed this until writing took me by the hand and showed me. In this way, writing can recast earlier perceptions, pluck the cloth off a long-hidden truth, provide a mode of self-reflection and revelation in the middle of life.

Do's and Don'ts of Automatic Writing

DO:

Go wherever your pen leads you
Write what feels easy
Write in the order that things occur to you
Stray off the path
Allow everything in
Be wild and messy

DON'T:

Wait for inspiration
Try to live up to some ideal
Edit, revise, or worry
Consider grammar or spelling
Reread what you've written
Compare
Judge
Justify
Explain

Here's Peter Elbow's classic description of why automatic writing can be so liberating:

The commonsense, conventional understanding of writing is as follows. Writing is a two-step process. First you figure out your meaning, then you put it into the language. Most advice we get either from others or from ourselves follows this model: first try to figure out what you want to say; don't start writing till you do, make a plan; use an outline; begin writing only afterward. Central to this model is the idea of keeping control, keeping things in hand. Don't let things wander into a mess. The commonest criticism directed at the process of writing is that you didn't clarify your thinking ahead of time; you allowed yourself to go ahead with fuzzy thinking; you allowed yourself to wander; you didn't make an outline. . . .

This idea of writing is backwards. That's why it causes so much trouble. Instead of a two-step transaction of meaning-into-language, think of writing as an organic, developmental process in which you start writing at the very beginning—before you know your meaning at all— and encourage your words gradually to change and evolve. Only at the end will you know what you want to say or the words you want to say it with. You should expect yourself to end up somewhere different from where you started. Meaning is not what you start out with, but what you end up with.

A Cautionary Tale

Here's a scenario that illustrates why freewriting can be so important:

A woman sits down to write what she has already determined will be a first-person fictional account based on an incident that took place when she was a teenager—the day she lost her virginity.

She's fairly sure that the account is going to be humorous; she knows not only how it's going to end but even the magazine she wants to submit it to.

In fact, she feels as if she's already written the piece in her mind; it's simply a matter of transcribing it. But the fact that she knows so much about it before the actual writing doesn't inspire but inhibits her. Soon she begins to dread sitting down and starting it at all.

What if she's disappointed? What if she can't make it come out as she's planned?

So she keeps thinking about it instead, jotting down notes and holding off work until weeks have gone by and she has nearly lost the impulse.

Finally one morning she makes herself sit down, and she rapidly writes the first page. She stops, rereads and edits, then begins the second page. But even as she writes, she is flooded with disappointment. This is not sounding as she imagined; it is not clever, fleet, and ironic, but serious, even melancholy. Worse, she feels the story slipping away from her and heading in a direction she didn't intend. Far from being humorous, her writing is veering into an upsetting area that she didn't intend to visit—a brother's illness.

She can't get the piece back on the track she wants. And she prohibits herself from following the path that tempts her. Dismayed, she gives up and finds excuses to avoid working on it further, thus prohibiting herself from seeing what her mind was tugging at her to reveal.

Automatic writing is often shot through with a potent freshness and unplanned beauty, a reminder of how the common language of ordinary life is so often full of poetry and drama.

From Rondell, a ten-year-old boy in a homeless shelter:

THE MOST BEAUTIFUL MAN ON EARTH
His name is Piano Teeth
He has megaphone ears
He has a bald spot and freckles

He wears the same clothes every day
He has knotty hair
He has an ugly bird
His bird has one eyebrow
His beauty is in his hands

From Edwin Richardson:

I was born in Georgia, in the country, where the dirt can be so red. My mother was seventeen and I was her second child. By the time she was twenty, she would have four children—me and my three sisters. (Later when I was thirteen, we would adopt a baby boy whose eyes were just as blue as ours. Twenty-three years later my brother would die of AIDS in an old house in Memphis with a closet full of beautiful dresses. My mother, so much older by then, would be with him, his nurse.)

From Mary Nyberg:

Running paths connect my life, as arteries running from my toes straight into my heart. Each time I return to a place of former residence, I run the old trails. It's like meeting old friends. I plan for it, crave it, and insist on doing it alone. Memories awaken in me as I recognize and anticipate each crack in a sidewalk or rock on a path. Usually everything is the same: the tree with a hollow trunk on Turtle Creek in Dallas, the spot where arrowheads abound in Giddings, Texas, the cold spot in the land on my family ranch, and the suddenly blue vision of the lake through the trees at Damsite Park in Arkansas . . . part of my soul has been left in these places. Returning, I reclaim some part of my whole that has escaped me, often rejuvenating my focus and understanding that I have grown beyond the past, still missing it all the same.

I've also had pages of startling material emerge from following a first thought that came out of nowhere—one that didn't even make sense at the time.

Here's an excerpt from an automatic piece of mine. I had no idea what to do with it—if anything. Later I found that it fit as the prologue to my book *White Girls*. This is not to suggest that automatic writing necessarily "becomes" something—think of it instead as a method of writing for enrichment, pleasure, and revelation—and therefore as always worthy.

Although none of us knew who he was then and most of us never learned later, we attended a grade school in Union, Ohio, named after Marcus Aurelius. His name became as common to us as Homer, a village to our east that specialized in bait, and Morocco, a town in Indiana where one of my aunts had moved when it became clear she'd never marry. We already had our view of Caesar, a pizza parlor on Calumet that specialized in lasagna, and the Forum, where we bought my orthopedic shoes. It was not our fault that at Marcus Aurelius, world history only went back to the Civil War, that our imaginations stopped at the Atlantic beaches near Maine. Still, even deep in Ohio, someone remembered the Parthenon, recalled a line from the *Iliad*, possessed a gene from the Roman Empire. Even deep in Ohio, with no water to look at, people bending in cornfields, standing on corners, were known to smell something salty and ancient and be inspired.

In actuality, my grade school was called Horace Mann elementary, I never had an aunt in Morocco, and Homer, a real town, doesn't specialize in bait, as far as I know. Later we'll discuss your tendency as a writer—whether you're pulled to try to tell the whole truth and nothing but the truth or if you can't help but lie (like me).

Writing with Prompts

Human beings are amazingly obedient creatures. Once learned, the rules and strictures of English classes years in the past still linger in us—hectoring us not to wander, to stick to the point, to not make a mess.

Writing automatically with prompts is a way to bypass these old rules and voices. It's a way to be bold and wild again. By allowing yourself to follow the pull of your unconscious, without judgment or censor, you arrive at surprising destinations.

Sometimes in the first pages of an essay or a book you sense the seeds of everything that's to come. And you often see this same phenomenon in automatic writing—a beautiful internal organization and structure that would have been impossible to derive from a more conscious method, a fascinating prologue of the writing to come.

Once you have a prompt, sit with a block of uninter-rupted time and write, beginning with the first thought that enters your mind and continuing for at least twenty minutes.

Continue even if you can't think of anything to say, even if you write: "I hate this. This is stupid." Keep going even if you veer wildly off track, even if you say incrimi-nating, ridiculous things. After at least twenty minutes, put away what you've produced without reading it until the next morning. Then take it out, reread it, and begin another session, picking up from where you stopped.

The best prompts are those that are given to you by someone else on the spot. Then the words can enter your mind fresh and trigger first responses that are unclouded by contemplation.

In lieu of this, try using the following list of prompts for your automatic sessions. Because their focus is on archetypal topics common to us all, they often yield potent results.

My mother told me . . .

My father believed . . .

When we sat down at the table . . .

If I could see . . . again . . .

I never told anybody . . .

I learned about sex . . .

I always wanted to . . .

I thought it was love, but . . .

My grandmother's name was . . .

The house I grew up in . . .

When I first saw the baby . . .

When he died . . .

I was always scared of . . .

The goal is to let yourself be guided by your writing, to let it take you by the hand and pull you into rooms of your house you may not recognize, onto floors you've never explored before.

Such writing is often telling you something, leading you somewhere—to your theme, your secret, your truth.

Pick an object from your past; try for the earliest you can remember. Choose something specific: a red-rubber-toed sneaker, a striped piece of fabric, a green plastic pail.

Ask yourself what's important about this object. Why did it fly out of the past into your mind? Does it signify a time, a place, a person? What does it connect to? What is underneath it?

Write down at least a dozen things this object stirs up in your mind. Reread them—they constitute the architecture of an event or story you want to write about. In this way your unconscious lays out a path for you to follow.

Pick one of these memories and begin freewriting, letting the words flow from you. Write anything that enters your mind, no matter how seemingly unrelated or irrational it seems.

Don't rewrite, look back, or worry about grammar or punctuation. Don't stop to reread what you've written or cross anything out.

Dawdle, wander, write in circles, veer off the margins: do all the things you've been told not to do. Fill at least three full pages with words.

CHAPTER 5

LIFE'S LADDER

Anyone who's survived childhood has enough to write about for the rest of his life.

—FLANNERY O'CONNOR

Lives do not serve as models, only stories do that. And it is a hard thing to make up stories to live by. We can only retell and live by the stories we have read or heard. . . . [T]hey may be read, or chanted, or experienced electronically, or come to us, like the murmurings of our mothers, telling us what conventions demand. Whatever their form or medium, these stories have formed us all.

—CAROLYN HEILBRUN

Among the old sheet music in our piano bench that most signified my mother's musical talents was "Meet Me in St. Louis," with Judy Garland on the cover. My mother not only looked like Judy Garland to me when she was young, but she was also a piano player and singer of light melodies. But these virtues—her dark good looks, her fleet handwork on the Steinway, her lilting voice—did not come into play in the daily life of a midwestern housewife.

"Meet Me in St. Louis" was not one of the songs I was pressed to play by my own piano teacher, Miss L. She disapproved of popular music, even *old* popular music, and kept me burrowed deep in the heavy, maroon-covered Methodist hymnal, where commands such as *andante* (tenderly) rarely came into play.

Having given up on this gift herself, my mother now pressed these lessons on me, as if to have me complete whatever musical expression had been halted in her.

But it was a futile prospect, a waste of summer Wednesdays when I would have been better off left to my own devices. Even simple backyard sitting, studying the grass growing between my legs or my own hot epidermis, with its sweet self-cooking smell, would have been more profitable than those trapped hours in Miss L's parlor.

But such leisure was not advised at that time for girls like me, just as long baths and heavy sports were warned against during menstruation. So during those years of active growth, when my bones lengthened and my face knit together, I sat through airless afternoons pumping pedals beside Miss L, trying to span my small paws over octaves and concentrate on the chords of "How Great Thou Art." What I was really pondering was what it meant for Miss L and her unmarried sister to live on their own in a town where such lives fell somewhere between blasphemous and pitiable. What did they do all evening while other women dressed their salads and fried? What did they do with the energy that other women burned off lugging laundry, or toddlers, or ministering to their husbands' desires?

Played music was the answer, duets to be exact, Miss L on the piano, her sister on the violin. I'd caught sight of them several evenings on the way home from the carryout for our weekly bologna: lit in the window in their old lady dresses, oblivious of me and everyone else in our soybean and refinery town.

The truth was that I was not made for the piano. In the beginning this was no problem, since Miss L believed any child could be molded with time. But once she saw that I'd never get better, she cooled her efforts. Adolescence was beginning to show on me, and her lectures on grace notes and pacing began to seep into other arenas—the unsightliness of gum chewing and the frivolity of nail polish—it weighed the nails down so!

Once it became clear she had lost her chance with me, the exclamation points fell off her penciled instructions. She gave up on my perfecting *War March of the Priests* (from *Athalie*). She stopped trying to convey what *allegro* (with dignity) might mean to a girl like me, more occupied with matching my bleeding madras outfits and straightening the persistent wave in my hair.

My eye was increasingly torn away from the sheet music, distracted by any bright movement out the window—trucks, birds, boys batting tennis balls in the court across the street.

My mother, sniffing the end, delayed it a while by sending me off with *115 Folk Songs in Big Notes* and a 1966 Motown anthology, so that for several weeks Miss L suffered through "Tit Willow" and "Celito Lindo" mixed with "Stop! In the Name of Love!"

But these were all delaying tactics; it was over and everyone knew it.

Finally my mother called Miss L to say that after seven years I was going to try my hand at something else—boys and sex, this turned out to be, though none of us could have known it at the time.

The first Wednesday that I didn't have Miss L sitting on my horizon, metronome tapping, loamy breath at my neck, was a turning point that felt like the largest liberation. Music—gone! Whole notes and grace notes and *moderato cantabile.*

Soon enough I'd also dropped out of the girls' choral society, tugging off my cardigan and stepping out of my maroon skirt, as well as disassembling for good the clarinet I'd blown desultorily through grade school.

Finally unencumbered, my brain could flatline over comic book plots and eye makeup shades, then back to comic book plots again. I could join the flat, gray march. Was I following the Midwest female path, a trail of seasoned bread crumbs that would lead me away from music to a domestic life?

I didn't know. I had to scorch my way through town and out of it before I could tell that it was another kind of music I was after, the music in the Grimm fairy tales my mother read to me back when I could sit still—the golden geese, the spinning wheels and sweet cakes, but mostly the stories: Rapunzel's daughter—lost!—because of a dish of rampion; a queen saving her child from the manikin only by guessing his name (*Caspar, Balthazar, Malchior,* she tried before she got it right: *Rumpelstiltskin*).

Such stories were driven deep in me as rivets, and formed not only the tales I would tell but the plots I would eventually live.

Words were the place of my heart's deep core, but I had
to leave Miss L before I could discover this.

Crossroads

Every life has its own moments of transition and self-
discovery. And it is these emotional and physical milestones
that we often write about, again and again.

Instead of looking at life as a series of traditional crossroads, such as birth or graduation, try dividing it into the
personal turning points that have cumulatively made you
who you are. By chronicling these transitional scenes,
you not only chart your history but begin turning your
experience into narrative.

One period of your life may be more heavily weighted
than another and infuse, even indirectly, all that you write.
One woman who had a tumultuous childhood found that
most of her turning points—from losing her mother to
being placed in an orphanage—were clustered in her first
six years. Not surprisingly, this was the period that dominated most of her writing. A man remained preoccupied
with the trauma of his parents' divorce when he was a
teenager; the theme of separation and loss was a thread
running through all he wrote.

In my own life, my early rebellion and the adoption of my daughter were two turning points that dominated my writing and my consciousness—which often end up being the same thing. What you write is often what is sitting there, in the foyer of your mind, tapping its foot, waiting to be attended to. My early dramas weighted my life so there was always this sagging spot at seventeen, no matter how old I became.

When I had back trouble in my thirties, I made an appointment with a "network" chiropractor. After I was laid out on his table, I was surprised to see that he wasn't going to actually touch me, but simply was holding his hands over different quadrants of my body, as if to sense my radiant heat.

He stopped when his hands were hovering over my midsection.

"What happened to you around sixteen or so? Did you have an accident or something—maybe break an arm or leg?"

I shook my head no; he hadn't asked about my heart, so I didn't tell him.

He didn't help my back, but he made me think about how we carry the central events of our lives within us, as Rilke said we carry our own deaths. They are notched deep inside us like the rings of trees.

Circling

We all have incidents we revisit, circling them like a dog looking for a place to rest. I've seen people get a glazed look when I tell them I'm still writing about the 1960s in Ohio. I can read the thoughts in the back of their eyes: *Why don't you move on? Haven't you dwelled on this enough?*

But even when I've forced myself to try something different—say, a mystery or even a poem—there is always a road I veer back to no matter who's in the driver's seat that leads straight to my teenage years, when I made the most noise and trouble, when I broke my own heart when no one else would do it for me. There's still something close to the bone that I haven't gotten right.

You're the only one who knows what is gnawing behind the drywall, trying to escape. You can try sidestepping it all you want, but it will keep at you until it finally comes out.

For example, when I first began writing about "Meet Me in St. Louis" I had planned to dwell on the way the title's emphatic command *Meet me!* struck some adventurous girlhood chord in me and how St. Louis seemed as exotic and far off as the moon. I did not know then that it was the gateway to the West, that its giant arch was the division between this and that, that it was on the banks of the Mississippi.

And further, I had intended to write about how the words *Meet Me in St. Louis* later took on great freighted meaning, when I flew there to meet my daughter, who had been moored all along in the vast state of Missouri, and that there were points in the future when I would actually say those very words or variants to her: *Let's meet in St. Louis,* or *See you in St. Louis,* and how remarkable this seemed. Or even more amazing, how it felt to go up in an elevator in a St. Louis hotel and see at the end of the hallway a tiny convergence of so much I've loved running toward me, all gilded ringlets and a face like the moon, calling me the most endearing of terms.

To be a grandmother and still have one! Maybe this was common in pockets of Appalachia, but I had known no one else to have this great good fortune—and without having done anything whatsoever to deserve it.

This is what I had intended to write, but I needed to write about Miss L for some reason, so I had to wait a little, and write it now.

Pivotal Points

Autobiographical crossroads and transitions are embedded in the work of all writers. The death of William Maxwell's mother from the Spanish influenza of 1918 turns up both as a central event and as an enduring thread of loss in his work. It's used in novelistic form in *They Came Like Swallows* and revisited in *So Long, See You Tomorrow*.

Edith Wharton's affair and subsequent divorce—and the underlying issues of female dependence and freedom from social convention—form the preoccupations of many of her fictional characters, from Lily Bart in *The House of Mirth* to Newland Archer in *The Age of Innocence*.

The abandonment Dickens felt so keenly as a result of a central incident in his early life, when his parents pulled him out of school and sent him to work full-time in a blacking warehouse, was a theme echoed throughout his career.

He wrote of this time:

> The deep remembrance of the sense I had of being utterly neglected and hopeless; of the shame I felt in my position; of the misery it was to my young heart to believe that, day after day, what I had learned, and thought, and delighted in, and raised my fancy and my emulation up by, was passing away from me, never to be brought back any more; cannot be written.

It could not be written in this snatch of autobiography perhaps, but Dickens was fully able to weave the pain of this pivotal event into the lives of the orphans and neglected children—Pip, Nicholas Nickleby, and others—who populated his novels.

List ten turning points in your life. These should be the pivotal moments that have most influenced who you are. Avoid the obvious, such as the day you got married or landed your first job, and go for the more deep and personal: the day you first got your period, the day you realized you were gay, the day you drove to the abortion clinic, the day you found out your father was cheating on your mother.

Consider the list.

If you had life to live over, what points would you change?

Which ones would you keep the same?

Pick the point that turned your life in a different direction.

Write automatically following the prompt: "It was a time when . . ."

SILENCING THE CRITICS

I am convinced that talent is almost a commonplace, something that almost everyone shares—as most people dream—but most people are inhibited by self-criticism before the event, so that many ideas are discarded or lost in transit between the brain and the manuscript. The great writer is doubtless one who allows all the things he thinks to pass into his writing. He has no tollkeeper at the gate, so to speak, allows even the seemingly ridiculous things to pass, tries to catch every nuance, every thought, knows that in the final form all things will be coherent. Between him and the fragmentary, unrealized writer there may be only this difference: that the latter has a very active tollkeeper, turning things back.

——MARGUERITE YOUNG

Almost anything you do will be insignificant, but it is very important that you do it.

——GANDHI

Writing can get you into trouble.

You can get into hot water from pillaging your loved ones, from conflating parents with strangers, from tossing boyfriends and brothers into a blender so you end up with a Cubist portrait—one person's eye here, another's leg there.

People don't like to be used, and who can blame them? But you might as well forget trying to calculate who might be offended by what you write. It's not only impossible, it's also enough to keep you from ever writing a word.

After I published my first book, I sat up nights trying to reread it from the perspective of my family, each word, every semifact, piercing their souls. I had done none of this during the actual writing: the words had flowed out like lava, hot and oblivious.

But now, set in type, punctuated, and ISBN'd, it felt as if I had pulled open every underwear drawer in the house.

It wasn't just that some of these stories were rooted in the truth, but that so many of them *weren't* and there was no way to inform the reader of this, to footnote, for example, that while a cleanup scene in the attic might be perfectly accurate, the episode where my mother had an affair with a milkman never happened at all.

And I was stunned by how I had snuffled up anything in my path—a grandfather's name, a brother's smile, and the careless, lazy way I'd only half altered the truth. Why change Jim Greggs only to Joe Briggs when I could so easily have made him Igor Lansing?

But I was off the hook, right? This was fiction. I checked the copyright page, the library sticker, as if to reassure myself.

But it didn't work. I still had nightmares of being disowned by my family, an archaic concept I'd never thought of before, even in my wildest days of rebellion.

Edna O'Brien says: "Any book that is any good must be, to some extent, autobiographical, because one cannot and should not fabricate emotions; and although style and narrative are crucial, the bulwark, emotion, is what finally matters."

Still, in workshops and elsewhere, I am struck by the apology and justification that infuses so much writing, especially female writing.

It wasn't so long ago that T. S. Eliot, among others, railed against the personal in writing, which prohibited much of what women—then mired in the domestic—had to say. This may seem an archaic notion, but I still find women so bound by these old prohibitions, so drenched in a legacy of anonymity and silence, that they are reluctant to write a word about themselves, even in the basement corner of a Dutch Reform church rec room, where no publisher or editor—let alone dead mother or vengeful ex-husband—would ever appear.

And then there's me. After my first book was published, I stressed how I hadn't *meant* to write a book at all, but had simply been haplessly writing stories that were occasionally published in the tiniest literary magazines, when out of the blue an editor swooped down from the sky and asked if I had more, and I said yes, I have a drawerful, and then she said send them, and I did, and she helped me arrange them, and I wrote an extra piece or two to make it all meld together, and—voilà—a book! Without trying.

This reminds me of the romance novels I used to scornfully edit, where the heroines were always stumbling around on their high heels, collapsing into a hero's arms, boneless and mute.

Implicit in this was that I wasn't *trying*, that I *hadn't meant to*, as if intentionality were itself a crime. You couldn't possibly want to have sex; you couldn't actually mean to write a book or say what you really felt.

A few months after my book had made a small, terrible splash in my hometown, where I'd convinced myself that no reading material besides the occasional romance or religious tract ever penetrated, I happened to be at my parents' house when an acquaintance of my mother's called to cajole her into attending a local dinner.

"I hope you're not avoiding it because you're embarrassed about your daughter's book," the woman said.

"Oh no," my mother replied without missing a beat. And then, "Anyway, it's fiction."

If anyone, my mother was in a position to know this. The mother in my books was far more provincial in every way than my real blood-and-sinew mother, who may have had roots in her, but had been worsened by my exaggerating ways.

The mother in my books represented the way mine felt to me in my teens, an unreliable period when anyone who places the slightest constraint on you seems fascist in the extreme.

But the woman who said this, who hung up the phone unaware of the fact that I had been listening in, was my *real* mother—the original rebellious daughter, who had typed in a basement office so I could go to college and later write the very kind of book she found herself defending.

It turned out that neither of my parents was so predictable after all, something I had been unable to see in my early myopia. They had taken the challenge of having me as a daughter (the midnight phone calls, the sheer small-town aversion to being noticed, my unrelenting incorrigibleness), and became something almost unheard of in a small place at a certain time—more liberal and various, far larger than where they were from.

They made me see how people are full of extraordinary possibilities simply waiting for the chance to emerge.

In fact, one of my characters got ahead of me in noticing this when he says: "Underneath small-town life lurked monumental possibilities, but the ground sometimes had to shift before they gave way."

In this mysterious way, characters in one's writing can sometimes see things far earlier and with greater clarity than you.

The Angel in the House

The conventional idea of writing is that you first figure out your meaning, then put it into language. In this version of how to write, there is always the tollkeeper, as Marguerite Young names him, or the editor or critic sitting beside you.

Virginia Woolf called this silencing presence the Angel in the House. In her famous essay, the Angel's wing throws a shadow over the writer's page as she tries to guide her pen, telling her to flatter, charm, and deceive with her words. It is the Angel who tries to "pluck the heart" out of her writing.

This creature often appears when a writer approaches an area freighted with deep feeling.

In her essay, Woolf talks about a woman writer who

was letting her imagination sweep unchecked round every rock and cranny of the world that lies submerged in the depths of the unconscious being. Now came the experience, the experience that I believe to be far commoner with women writers than with men. The line raced through the girl's fingers. Her imagination had rushed away. It had sought the pools, the depths, the dark places where the largest fish slumber. And then there was a smash. There was an explosion. There was foam and confusion. The imagination had dashed itself against something hard. The girl was roused from her dream. She was indeed in a state of the most acute and difficult distress. To speak without figure she had thought of something, something about the body, about the passions which it was unfitting for her as a woman to say. Men, her reason told her, would be shocked. The consciousness of what men will say of a woman who speaks the truth about her passions had roused her from her artist's state of unconsciousness. She could write no more. The trance was over. Her imagination could work no longer. . . .

You don't have to be a woman to be well acquainted with the Angel.

She's the voice at your shoulder who'd rather you remain silent.

She's the presence behind your procrastination, excuse-making, and fear.

SHE'S THE ONE WHO WHISPERS:

If I write,
I'll hurt my family, my lover, my friends
I won't measure up
I'll find out I have no talent
I'll look like a fool
I'll discover what I really feel

Writer Lynne Sharon Schwartz has said that you can't be a good girl and a writer, and you can't be a good boy either.

The kind of writing I'm encouraging won't allow restraint or caution. It will show you what you mean instead of the other way around. You have the rest of your life to edit and rewrite and change slanderous material if you need to. Getting the words down is the difficult task, and you have to get out of your own way—and get everyone else out of your way—to allow this to happen.

I have seen over and over the difference between the willed, critical, ambitious *I want to be good* voice and the other voice, linked to the unconscious, your middle-of-the-night voice when you are writing in your diary and expect no one to see it.

Writing can be dreadful if you never catch a glimpse of the second one.

Francine du Plessix Gray says:

The first thing we must do when we set out to write is to shed all narcissism. My own decades of fear came from my anxiety that my early drafts were ugly, sloppy, not promising enough. We must persevere and scrawl atrocities, persevere dreadful draft after dreadful draft in an unhindered stream of consciousness, persevere, if need be, in the technique of automatic writing. And within that morass of words there may be an ironic turn of phrase, a dislocation, that gives us a key to the voice, the tone, the structure we're struggling to find.

Writing about the Body

Many of us have special difficulty writing candidly about sex and the body. This is when the Angel of the House swoops down most often and takes control of our pens.

The only place many of us have read about this topic is in romances. And nowhere is the lack of truth-telling more striking than in these kinds of stories, where women are portrayed as passive, infantile, bumbling, and frantic for love—any love. And men as virile, commanding ciphers.

Consider the ramifications of a steady diet of this:

FROM *Promise Me Forever* BY JANELLE TAYLOR

Flames of desire leapt through Rachel's body. She had never experienced anything like this with any man. She yearned to give free rein to the emotions, to let them sweep her away. She couldn't, though, not yet. She didn't want to give Dan the worst—a wicked—impression of her. She decided the best path of escape was to go limp in his embrace as if she'd passed out. . . .

"Don't be afraid of me, Rachel," Dan said. "I would never hurt you." Rachel fretted that she wouldn't know how to respond correctly, how to please him. What if she froze up as with her third husband, Phillip? What if it hurt or became rough as with her second husband, Craig?

She murmured, "I don't know what to do, so you'll have to tell me or show me."

His fingers caressed her cheek. "There's plenty of time to teach you anything you don't know."

Now consider how startling it is to read Jamaica Kincaid's take on a physical liaison that feels like an honest account of a woman's reaction, stripped of artifice:

His name was Hugh. I liked the sound of his voice, not because it reminded me of anything in particular—I just liked it. I liked his eyes—they were a plain brown. I liked his mouth and imagined it kissing me everywhere; it was just an ordinary mouth. I liked his hands and imagined them caressing me everywhere; they were not unusual in any way. . . .

As soon as we met, we spoke only to each other. Nothing we said to each other was meant to leave a lasting impression. . . . He kissed me on my face and ears and neck and in my mouth. If I enjoyed myself beyond any-thing I had known so far, it must have been because such a long time had passed since I had been touched in that way by anyone; it must have been because I was so far from home. I was not in love.

Slaying the Angel

My own early writing erupted out of such desperation that for a long time the Angel in the House didn't seem to apply to me. But she swooped down when it was time for my first book to be published, assailing me with belated guilt and remorse. She didn't say how could you *write* this so much as how could you *publish* it?

But I had such an urge to try to write truthfully about my life—not necessarily the literal truth but the emotional truth, a topic we'll discuss later—and I was so gratified to have my work appreciated that in the end I was able to silence my fears.

Still, since then I have made the Angel's more frequent acquaintance.

If I'm not careful, I find her slipping under the door.

Her voice of belittlement and discouragement has to be continually battled; it never stays away for long.

If you publish one book, she says you'll never write a second.

If you write fifty-one poems, she says you'll never write a fifty-second.

She says, *Who cares what you have to say? Who do you think you are anyway?*

So what to do about the Angel?

Here are some ways to ward her off:

- Write automatically and regularly so it becomes a habit, not a big production.

  Walter Mosley says: "If you want to be a writer, you have to write every day. The consistency, the monotony, the certainty, all vagaries and passions are covered by this daily recurrence.

  "You don't go to a well once but daily. You don't skip a child's breakfast or forget to wake up in the morning. Sleep comes to you each day, and so does the muse."

- Don't put off writing for another day, when you're feeling surer or happier or when you have more time. Do it now.

  Audre Lorde says: "I was going to die, if not sooner than later, whether or not I had ever spoken myself. My silences had not protected me. Your silence will not protect you."

- Stop writing when you're feeling good—such as in the middle of a paragraph you like—so that you can plunge right back in with pleasure when you begin again.

- Make believe you're writing to someone close to you and tell that person what you want to say.

- Skip hard patches; write out of sequence.

- Don't talk about writing or tell people your writing plans . . . just do it.
- Read other people: good rich writing is nourishing to the soul.
- Pay attention to what comes to you unbidden; write it down immediately; otherwise it'll vanish.
- Feed yourself; do the things that give you pleasure. Go to a museum, listen to music, spend time in nature.
- Go out into the world and pay attention to what's around you.
- Love as much as you can.
- Finally, don't write expecting acclaim or love or money; it puts too much weight on what you do.

> "Why do we seek fame?" a student asked the spiritual teacher Krishnamurti, according to *Think on These Things*.
>
> "Have you ever thought about it?" he responded. "We want to be famous as a writer, a poet, as a painter, as a politician, as a singer or what you will. Why? Because we don't really love what we are doing. If you loved to sing, or to paint, or to write poems— if you really loved it—you would not be concerned about whether you are famous or not. Our present education is rotten because it teaches us to love success and not what we are doing. The result has become more important than the action."

Still, being listened to can be an important component of personal writing. There's no denying that some of us *need* to share our work and have it publicly heard.

M was a young woman in her middle thirties who was burning with words when she whirred into one of my workshops in her motorized wheelchair. She had been born with cerebral palsy, then later had a stroke. It was hard to imagine the pith she had to muster to simply arrive at the classroom door.

She could speak in a fashion, but until you got to know her, it could be difficult to understand, and a comment might take a long, painful while to complete. But I usually let her try, stopping the class—a group of impatient, callow undergraduates—just so they could consider how arduous trying to be heard could be.

This may have been time-consuming, but the fact that she came at all was such a testament—to the ramps and special van, and the mother waiting out in the hall with her pocketbook.

But M didn't want to be an inspiration. She didn't want special treatment; she just wanted to be heard.

All the vivaciousness, spunk, and verve trapped in her came out in poetry that was feisty, religious, pissed-off, and romantic, a surprising, Emily Dickinson-like stew.

Once the class was over, she gathered her work together and had it bound in a paperback that she sold and gave to friends. At one public reading, she was pushed to the lectern to sit beside me while I read her poems, and if a human could be said to glow, she did. It was like having a golden nugget, a fallen star, a chunk of meteorite at my side.

She was a sponge, soaking up the recognition that these words had come from her, were embedded in her, whether or not you had ever heard her utter them.

There is no diminishing the power of this kind of attention—some of us need it more than others. And you can't help but feel that some of us deserve it more, too.

Look back at yourself as a child. Find a photo of yourself and study it.

Who was this little person?

What was told to you about your birth and childhood?

Where were you in the photo? What were you doing? Who is in the background/back story of this moment?

Now initiate a session of time travel. Imagine yourself walking over a bridge into the time and place of this photograph.

Write from the voice of this child, describing where you are, what you smell and see and feel.

CHAPTER 7

DEEPENING

I read first drafts as a mystery which drops clues to the riddle of my feelings, like a culprit who wishes to be apprehended . . . waiting for the real subject to reveal itself.

—PATRICIA HAMPL

Make the process of writing into atomic fission, setting off a chain reaction, putting things into a pot to percolate, getting words to take on a life of their own. Writing is like trying to ride a horse which is constantly changing beneath you, Proteus changing while you hang on to him. You have to hang on for dear life, but not hang on so hard that he can't change and finally tell you the truth.

—PETER ELBOW

Diving Down

To use the process of automatic writing to its fullest, you need to surface, get your bearings, then dive in again, plunging down even deeper.

This is the stage where you find the beating heart in your writing: the place where chaos begins to take shape, when memory, desire, and the unconscious begin to pulse and combine.

Amy Tan says:

After my mother died, I began to rewrite the novel I had been working on for the past five years. I wrote with the steadfastness of grief. My editor and dear friend, the great Faith Sale, would have called that grief "finding the real heart of the story." My mentor, Molly Giles, said the bones were there, I just had to reassemble them in a new way. To find that heart and repair the bones, I had to break them into pieces, then start to dig.

A common tendency in writing that has not yet deepened is to tell rather than show.

"It was an old town" is a telling sentence, but in this passage from *To Kill a Mockingbird,* Harper Lee *shows* us one:

Maycomb was an old town, but it was a tired old town when I first knew it. In rainy weather the streets turned to red slop; grass grew on the sidewalks, the courthouse sagged in the square. Somehow, it was hotter then: a black dog suffered on a summer's day; bony mules hitched to Hoover carts flicked flies in the sweltering shade of the live oaks on the square. Men's stiff collars wilted by nine in the morning. Ladies bathed before noon, after their three-o'clock naps, and by nightfall were like soft teacakes with frostings of sweat and sweet talcum.

Here Dave Marcon, a workshop participant, shows in all its terrible detail the accident that changed his life:

I never told anybody about my motorcycle accident in 1985 that left me permanently disabled. I was only twenty-two years old at the time. I became disabled after running into a Safeway shopping cart that was left in the middle of Bay Street one night while I was driving home without a helmet in San Francisco's Marina District. I was knocked unconscious and the left side of my body was paralyzed. I sustained significant damage to the frontal, parietal, sensory, and cognitive areas of my brain when it ricocheted off the inside of my cranium when my left brow struck the curb at Bay and Laguna Streets. Someone parked in a van saw the accident and phoned 911. An ambulance took me to San Francisco General Hospital where I spent one month in intensive care in a coma.

Another way to show rather than tell is to locate a specific episode or scene of significance and dramatize it, using dialogue and detail.

Instead of stating that the character of Birdie was a bitter woman disillusioned by marriage, Lillian Hellman dramatizes this in a scene from *The Little Foxes*:

Alexandra: Why did you marry Uncle Oscar?

Birdie: I don't know. I thought I liked him. He was kind to me and I thought it was because he liked me too. But that wasn't the reason— (*Wheels on Alexandra*) Ask why *he* married *me*. I can tell you that: he's told it to me often enough.

Addie (*leaning forward*): Miss Birdie, don't—

Birdie (*speaking very rapidly, tensely*): My family was good and the cotton on Lionnet's fields was better. Ben Hubbard wanted the cotton and (*rises*) Oscar Hubbard married it for him. He was kind to me, then. He used to smile at me. He hasn't smiled at me since. Everybody knew that's what he married me for. (*Addie rises*) Everybody but me. Stupid, stupid me.

What It's Like

There's nothing like a deft description, a metaphor or simile to crack open the consciousness, to reveal all at once the particularity of a person or to evoke a world.

Coming up with what things are like has always been a great pleasure to me—the hoof that's pink as a pig's foot, the hair the color of cardboard, the voice that lifts like a skirt. Similes are my favorites, and in a single section of Jeffrey Eugenides' *Middlesex*, three seared into my mind:

They [boys] cover you like a sarcophagus lid. And call it love.

He stroked and squeezed while his lower half swished like a crocodile's tail.

Her red hair flapped like a gale warning.

Metaphors and similes remind us of the power of language to take an ordinary experience and preserve it forever. After reading a good one, you may never look at something the same way again.

The challenge is not to *try* for these devices but to *open* up to them and the way they signal the relatedness and interconnection of elements in the world.

In this same way, a vivid description can toss a character right into the room with you: There she is again, Mrs. Edith Hutt, your old Sunday school teacher, with her underbite and eye twitch and big black purse. There she is in her Dacron dress and damp armpits.

Writing deeply and concisely brings you closer to what's right in front of you.

Capturing the particularity of a scene or person can be so stirring, so affecting, that it can take you by the hand and lead you to another place.

I've had the experience of remembering something so deeply and in such detail—in one case, a green suede coat with white acrylic lining—that right behind it, almost attached to the sleeve like a mitten, trailed a chunk of time and a story.

Details of evocation can lead you back in time and allow you to capture lost worlds. As you write, close your eyes and resituate yourself on the hot car seat, in the weedy backyard, in the person's arms you're trying to summon up. Smell the English Leather, taste the rhubarb pie, turn your face to the northeasterly wind.

I've tried to do this with the now vanished back bedroom in my grandmother's house, with its button drawers and fabric remnants, the cool green plaster walls, the wedding pictures in the half-light.

The way it felt waking up in her narrow bed to the scent of percolating coffee and cinnamoned baking, the exhale of laundry churning hot and sweet in the background.

The talcumed sweat in the crook of her neck as she hugged me, the prototype, the original hug of every other to come.

Evoking this is a way of holding on to her, though she's now in a nursing home, hoisted with chains and pulleys. It is a way of enthroning her in the palace of the mind.

Details can bring the most ordinary memory alive and stir great feeling.

The following is from William Maxwell's *Time Will Darken It:*

Between quarter to two and quarter past three an age of quiet passed over the house on Elm Street, over the richness contained in cupboards, the serenity of objects in empty rooms. The front stairs creaked, but not from any human footstep. The sunlight relinquished its hold on the corner of an oriental rug in the study in order to warm the leg of a chair. A fly settled on the kitchen ceiling. In the living-room a single white wheel-shaped phlox blossom hung for a long time and then dropped to the table without making a sound. On a dusty beam in the basement a spider finished its web and waited. Just when the arrangement of the furniture, the disposition of light and shadow, the polish and sweet odour of summer seemed final and the house itself a preserved invaluable memory, Ab awoke and called out to her mother.

It is not only the majesty of Maxwell's writing that makes this passage so beautiful, but the details—the phlox blossom, and the sweet odor of summer. . . .

Details are definite and concrete when they appeal to the senses. But when you are deepening, you want details that are significant as well.

Loading on descriptors like sour cream on a baked potato isn't the point; any computer can generate a florid sentence full of cornflower blue eyes and piercing gazes and orgasms of exploding stars.

Saying that a door was deep red may be concrete, but saying that the door was "a lacquered Chinese red, so luminous that it shone like a ruby" conveys meaning as well, that the door was beckoning, inviting, and luxurious.

Buried Treasure

Deepening is a long-term process; often you have to write and live and write some more before you reach your buried treasure, before you find the illuminating connections, patterns, and preoccupations that fuel your work.

Some incidents require a certain distance—years of turning, sifting, digging—before you can fully apprehend them. But that doesn't mean you should sit back on your haunches and wait until you're wise. Plunge in now. Try to get at it in today's way, whatever that may be. It's often in the seeds of what doesn't "work" that you later find what will.

Writer Tony Kushner claimed the impetus for writing his play *Angels in America* came from a poem he'd written ten years earlier, then rediscovered.

There's a painful incident from my past that I've been writing about—and trying to comprehend—for nearly thirty years, and I'm trying still.

This is why it's so essential to approach writing as a long-term exploration.

Here's how Anna Muenster, a physician from a workshop, put it:

The greatest and most astonishing discovery I have made since the age of eighty is that the loss of neurons from the age of thirty-five on, which limits storage of recent events as one gets older, seems to bring into focus with more clarity the significance of earlier events, some never before remembered or thought of until this stage of life. Different strands come together and suddenly present connections among otherwise disparate and far-apart events, giving meaning and pointing to purposes not sensed before.

Pick a stranger who intrigues you—the woman who walks down your street and picks through the garbage; the long-haired boy who Rollerblades through downtown.

Now imagine his or her life. Invent a name, a location, a background. Delve under the skin.

On one piece of paper, write a short descriptive history of this life, where you present specific facts, such as: "Ella Franklin was a nurse, born in Lansing, Michigan, who had a stroke at the age of sixty-two and never found another job."

On another sheet, write a scene from this life and dramatize it. Have the character speak out in dialogue in an episode that illuminates some aspect of who she is.

CHAPTER   8

TELLING THE TRUTH

Lying with one's body and one's words is, among the oppressed, a dreadful necessity.

—ADRIENNE RICH

Four years after Adrienne Rich published her first book, I read it in almost disbelieving wonder: someone my age was writing down my life. I felt then, as I feel now, that for each reader there are only a few poets of whom that is true, and by the law of averages, those poets are usually dead or at least far removed in time and space. But here was a poet who seemed, by a miracle, a twin: I had not known till then how much I had wanted a contemporary and a woman as a speaking voice in my life.

—HELEN VENDLER

What does it mean when you can't remember what's true anymore, when the stories you've told are so well worn and revisited that they're seared in your brain, true and false alike?

That's what's happened to me.

I feel sure, for example, that I called my daughter's father when he was stationed in Vietnam, just after I'd returned, empty-handed, from a home for unwed mothers in the summer of 1969.

But while I can see myself doing this—standing in a phone booth, dressed in a yellow plaid skirt, holding a piece of lined paper, I'm not sure what happened next.

It was still easy to manipulate telephones in the late 1960s. I had already perfected a method of listening in to party-line conversations of neighborhood housewives, who dragged their cords behind them as they swept or ironed.

I'd developed a light breath, a method of putting the receiver down just so, using a washrag. I did this so well that I rarely heard the dread *Is someone else on this line?*

Phone scams were easy when operators were local sisters and cousins who could be coaxed into interrupting a boyfriend's protracted conversation if you claimed there was an emergency ("My mother's in labor!") or to charge your call to someone else's line.

In my storytelling mind, I did this: stood dressed in one of the skirt sets my mother had mixed and matched in anticipation of my reentry into normal teenage life and made the call, using a dime and charging it to someone else's random line.

I can hear the succession of operators as they clicked me further, deeper, uttering codes until, in the hissing, reverberating distance, a man's gruff voice replied in a slur of militarese.

This was Vietnam; this was a jungle I couldn't have located even if we'd owned a map of the world.

My boyfriend had departed for this spot the same season I'd left for the unwed mothers' home: he on a transport plane, me in a slow-moving car. We'd both inched out of our hometown, two specks on the horizon, already estranged.

He had wanted to leave our baby back in his neighborhood for his sisters and mother to raise. Given my youth and callowness, my side had viewed adoption as the best option. No one—myself included—had thought it a good idea to consign a baby to me.

But while I remember standing in the phone booth on that day in August, I don't remember whether my boyfriend actually came to the phone. I can't be sure whether that final connection was ever made.

In my storytelling mind, though, he always answered, and I told him—everything. All the measurements that only a partner in reproduction would want to know: my poundage at the end of pregnancy (147!), and that of our phantom baby; the length of my labor and of the incision the doctors made.

And even more importantly, in my storytelling mind, he always listened, connected to me by wires that lay under fathomless oceans, that sizzled the soil in the jungle where I imagined him: shorn and gangly, holding a rifle like the one he'd kept in the back of his Chevy when he was a Black Panther and drove me through the imperialist infrastructure of our hometown.

In the end, this is the only fact I am completely sure of—that you could have seen us driving through the back streets of our Ohio hometown for that one burning season—aimlessly, we thought, but in truth following the bumpy, potholed road of fate.

Which Truth?

I'm not the only one who has trouble holding on to the truth. Neuroscientists say our memories are actually memories of memories. So how can you ever approach the truth?

It depends on the one you're trying to grasp.

Actual truth is a factual account of events as they happened, your tenth-birthday party as recorded on video, complete with dialogue.

The rough truth is when you remember that something occurred, let's say an argument in your dorm room, but you can only recall bits of it, let's say the glass you smashed in the heat of battle. Maybe other people present remember additional parts of the argument, and you can cobble together a fairly good representation of the event.

But the emotional truth—coming up with the conversation you wish you'd had with your father on one of the many nights he returned home drunk—is something else. When you begin to wade into this arena, you're entering the realm of fiction.

Facts often become better or worse when transposed into fiction—usually worse. I come from a small town, which I shrank down even further, to the way it felt to me when I was young. I made my alter ego, Loretta, as brave as I wish I had been, and her parents much more provincial than mine ever were.

But whenever I try to explain this, I sound either foolish or pompous, or as if I'm lying even more. People insist on acting as if fiction is true, and maybe they are correct in doing so—because the truth that fiction reveals is the emotional truth—perhaps the one that matters most of all.

Lying vs. Exaggerating

Because memory can never be pinned down exactly, all writers have to invent. The question is, how much.

I find it challenging to write the actual truth, and when I try, it has a different sound.

Here's an example from an essay of mine, "A Love Diverted":

My boyfriend was another casualty of my pregnancy; three of us were lost, in all. Although he offered marriage, I took this only as a courteous gesture and declined his mother's offer to keep the baby, convinced that it would be the same as keeping it myself. There were hard feelings after that; and a separation; I received a phone call from him occasionally, usually on the birthday of our child. He always believed we would find our daughter, even though I—the one who made sporadic searches—remained doubtful. He prayed for this, he told me; along with his mother, for whom I had developed a soft spot.

He had done what I had done, what you seem to do when you have a child with someone and all is lost—he romanticized our past. That our relationship had only lasted a few months, that he had originally been more interested in a girlfriend of mine than in me, that half the nights I spent at his house were with his mother, listening to her tell stories and eating her cake—these facts became lost to us, glossed over by surplus feelings; the conception of our daughter had gathered around itself a holy, redemptive light. Who had known what a monumental act we were performing behind the shower curtain of his bedroom, when instead of algebra, we turned and studied ourselves. Neither of us could help what we did with such material later. For a long time he constructed a fantasy of what the two of us had been to each other. And for twenty years, using various voices and angles of approach, I wrote about that window of time.

When I wrote about these same events in fiction, which I did for years before I reconnected with my daughter, I was involved in what I describe above. I took my surplus feelings and infused my relationship with drama, turning and twisting it into fiction.

Under Loretta's influence, during the time they'd been together, Luther'd begun to imagine a future of vague glory, where, without much effort, he'd right things, turn the world around. After they made love, he'd occasionally talk about these things with her, not only because she seemed the type who'd want to hear them, but because the simple act of their lying together still felt almost revolutionary to him.

"You'll do something, I know you will," Loretta would say afterwards, lying in the drafty rooms of their spent love, and Luther'd try to forget that she'd been dozing through most of his talk, that even as he was speaking, she had the full intention of leaving shortly, of driving home in her father's Buick, equipped with climate control and full of premium gas, to a house so soundly designed, so carefully decorated, that no one, neither she nor he, believed that the life in it, nor what it signified, would ever fall or crumble.

In real life, I never made these comments; nor do I have any reason to think that such thoughts were in my old boyfriend's mind. I did this fictionalizing unconsciously, for my own purposes. Underneath it all was the desire to elevate my brief relationship to the status of a significant romance—for it *must* have been significant; it had resulted in our vanished daughter, who in her absence shone and bewitched us.

Re-imagining

It is easy to discern the autobiographical truthfulness embedded in so much writing, from Elizabeth Bishop's plaintive poetry to Alice Munro's disaffected Canadian narrator wives.

With so many first-person narrators and plots that parallel the writer's life—why not just call these works nonfiction, say they are "true" and be done with it?

Because something else is at work; a "re-imagination" is how Lorrie Moore puts it, in describing the process she used to write such stories as "People Like That Are the Only People Here," which chronicles a mother's ordeal in facing her baby's cancer, a story that reportedly echoes events in her real life. The story reads so realistically, right down to the mother being a fiction writer and the husband/father urging her to take notes of their terrible process:

> "Take notes," says the Husband, after coming straight home from work, midafternoon, hearing the news and saying all the words out loud—*surgery, metastasis, dialysis, transplant*—then collapsing in a chair in tears. "Take notes. We are going to need the money."
>
> "Good God," cries the Mother. Everything inside her suddenly begins to cower and shrink, a thinning of bones. Perhaps this is a soldier's readiness, but it has the whiff of death and defeat. It feels like a heart attack, a failure of will and courage, a power failure: a failure of everything.

In an interview, although Moore acknowledges a slight autobiographical element in this story, she insists that it wasn't memoir. "It was fiction. . . . Things did not happen exactly that way. I re-imagined everything. And that's what fiction does. Fiction can contain real-life events and still be fiction."

This is part of the magic and mystery of writing: how we take our lives and use them for our own deep reasons, working them until they make sense, until they reveal what we need to understand or bear.

Think of your body as a map marked by the physical events of your lifetime—pleasures, illnesses, accidents, births.

List five central episodes from the life of your body: the day you miscarried a baby; the day you had your heart operated on or your breast biopsied. Pick the episode that stirs you most and write automatically for twenty minutes, allowing your body to do the talking.

CHAPTER 9

FINDING YOUR FORM

Fiction is storytelling. It doesn't mean that the story has to be about imaginary events. It doesn't make any difference whatsoever if the events actually happened to actual people or were made up. It's the use you put them to that makes them fiction.

——WILLIAM MAXWELL

There are some books that refuse to be written. They stand their ground, year after year, and will not be persuaded. It isn't because the book is not there and worth being written——it is only because the right form for the story does not present itself. There is only one right form for a story, and if you fail to find that form the story will not tell itself. You may try a dozen wrong forms but in each case you will not get very far before you discover that you have not found the right one.

——MARK TWAIN

Fiction writing is lying, put to socially acceptable if unprofitable use. It is one of several skills—such as eavesdropping and spying—that can be profitable for a writer.

I wish I'd known this earlier in my life, when I squandered lies instead of saving them up for good use.

Once, chasing a so-called boyfriend through the rural countryside, I swerved off the road in my mother's Chevy and ended up in a ditch, underneath barbed wire. Just beyond was a stretch of cornfield and my boyfriend's sports car, speeding away toward the horizon.

Even though I was sure he'd seen me, he did not turn back, and such was the state of our sad affair that I didn't even expect it.

He had already mistreated me in a catalogue of ways that amazed as much as hurt me. But what did I know? Maybe all men stood you up and made you chase them. (My father and grandfather didn't, but they didn't count in this sense.)

By the time I backed out of the ditch that day, the hood of the car was raked by barbed wire and the undercarriage caked with mud. Something was beginning to smoke under the hood, but I ignored this and turned the car south, toward home.

When I pulled up to our house, I walked in the back door and called out to my mother, "You better come see this," as if I were about to show her some natural wonder.

She followed me to the doorway and stood gazing out at the smoking car, *her* car, which she had financed and vacuumed and paid for by sitting for months, even years, in an office.

Before she could speak, I said, all in one breath:

"Sara wanted me to drive to the party, so I parked in her driveway, and by the time we got back this is what'd happened. She thinks Doug Lipton next door must have done it because I wouldn't dance with him last week at the teen center and because her brother threatened to call the cops if he kept growing pot in his backyard."

I stopped, panting like our dog. None of this explained the mud on the undercarriage or the smoking hood, but my mother wasn't exactly keeping track.

She looked abject, peering out at the car and, further, to my grisly future. Neither of us knew what she'd done to deserve me.

In this case, as in so many others, the truth would not have done. Even if my jaw had been prized open, I could not have admitted to my mother that I had backed under the limbo bar lower than she could have imagined, that there seemed to be some defect in me, some blank spot or broken cord, that enabled me to be mistreated so young.

I couldn't say any of this, or anything near it.

Only an omniscient observer, striding out of the Bible, would have been able to tell the truth.

And there had been other lies, far stranger:

Telling a boyfriend's neighbor that I was mulatto, in an odd foreshadowing of the daughter I'd produce myself.

Saying a fictitious family member had died as an excuse to quit a three-week stint as a surly waitress at Howard Johnson, then receiving a funeral spray of red gladiolas at my parents' house the next day.

Some lies may have even saved me:

Like the day a gas station attendant opened the door of the station bathroom with his key on a stick, then backed me into the dirty sink with his bulging trousers.

"You don't have to do this," I told him. "If you just give me a minute, I'll meet you in the car." (He left; I fled.)

Or saying I was three months pregnant when two men I'd hitchhiked with took me to a gravel quarry and tried to toss me into the backseat. This was a specific though not very original lie; still, it worked. (Why I was hitchhiking in the first place was another story, precipitated by yet another lie.)

It was only when I started writing fiction that I found a way to put this pathology to use, along with so many other antisocial tendencies.

It was no problem now, it might even be an asset, how I twisted things around, inflated and changed them, to the way they could have, perhaps the way they *should* have, been.

Even my free-form rebellion helped in this odd, non-profit endeavor. I could make a mess now, forget the rules, and sometimes end up with a revelation.

The great benefit of fiction is that it doesn't have to be fair or evenhanded; its great drawback is that, unlike life, it has to add up, to make sense somehow.

With fiction, you might start in the land of the real, but at some point you have to jump off the ledge, try your wings and fabricate.

You may be writing a perfectly truthful account of a banquet you once attended, describing the roast beef and turkey, but then you throw in Swedish meatballs that weren't there and give the waitress a lisp and a run in her stocking, and turn the woman who was sitting beside you, minding her own business, into a man with a Texas drawl.

If you find yourself veering off in this way for no apparent reason, then fiction is probably the place for you.

Resurrecting the Real

On the other hand, if you feel a loyalty to the facts of things—if you feel dishonest adding the lisp or the meatballs, then you belong in the land of nonfiction, where the goal is to resurrect the real.

Nonfiction stems from the impulse to capture what *is* or *was:* the firefly in the mayonnaise jar, the gardenia in the diary, the curl of hair in the locket.

Even so, you *still* have to invent—we know Truman Capote wasn't hiding in the backseat transcribing the conversations of the murderers for *In Cold Blood.*

There's no way Erik Larson could *precisely* know the exact moves of the murderous doctor and his victim, let alone their thoughts, in a Chicago house in the late 1890s. But how well he imagines them, nonetheless, in his nonfiction book *The Devil in the White City:*

Holmes offered Julia a cheerful "Merry Christmas" and gave her a hug, then took her hand and led her to a room on the second floor that he had readied for the operation. A table lay draped in white linen. His surgical kits stood open and gleaming, his instruments laid out in a sunflower of polished steel. Fearful things: bonesaws, abdomen retractor, trocar and trepan. More instruments, certainly, than he really needed, and all positioned so that Julia could not help but see them and be sickened by their hard, eager gleam.

He wore a white apron and had rolled back his cuffs. Possibly he wore his hat, a bowler. He had not washed his hands, nor did he wear a mask. There was no need.

She reached for his hand. There would be no pain, he assured her.

I also know there is no way for me to ever entirely capture an afternoon I spent with my grandfather in 1967—not unless it was caught on videotape—and even the record of our flickering images, our voices overlapping, could never take into account other facts of equal significance—his mood that day, the way the sky looked, how his face sat on the front of his head.

The smell of his electrician's uniform—the scent of electricity itself—the Aqua Velva on his neck. His whole back story, including his father, who laid himself out in the cemetery when he got drunk to make sure he'd fit in his plot.

How my grandfather sprayed county roads for a living, back when dust was a problem, before he became entranced by electricity's secret wires. His ruefulness, the minor chord of him, traveling first through my mother before piercing me.

The grandfather I'll dream of all my life, especially after

he dies, reminding me that he is still here—I only thought he'd vanished—residing in an infirmary on the other side of town.

How can I convey all this?

How can it be written down?

Even if every memory were raked together, even if I took affidavits and studied home movies, where the dead eat picnics with the living, I still couldn't capture the absolute truth, it would still fly from my hands.

All any of us can do is approximate, open the pantry and take words from jars so old and dusty that the corroded lids can barely be pried off.

We can take them from the yellowed newsprint lining the pantry, from books once borrowed from the cramped Ohio Bookmobile, spewing exhaust at the end of the block.

Who knows where the words come from, but we snatch them—all of us—and try to fashion what we feel and mean, not so much so that someone else might understand us, but so that we might understand ourselves.

The Good Hour

We all have our tendencies—toward fact or fiction—but we need the time and space to cultivate them, to even know what we're yearning toward.

Curiosity and invention take time, and modern life is built around the rushing exterior. It's perfectly possible to spend most of life on automatic pilot, without the space or inclination to note a flower's face or to raise your gaze up from the asphalt to consider a star.

You may not be able to seize the day, but try to give yourself the good hour when you slow down and open the lens of your eye to take in the world. Look at people's teeth and the shoes they wear and the way their ears attach to the sides of their heads. Consider what a catalpa leaf looks like, the complex knots of a spiderwort seedpod.

Savor words themselves—catalpa! spiderwort!—hold them in your mouth like caramels, write them down.

Peek under the skirt of someone else's life; try to imagine what it's like to be the Salvadoran maid sweating on the corner. Does she miss her mountains? Her mother? How did she end up all the way in Edison, New Jersey, and why?

Encourage in yourself what modern life discourages— curiosity is good for us and vital not only for writing but for living fully in the world.

Be Aware

Pay attention to the form that appeals to you, since it's usually a clue to the way you want to go in your own writing.

Form can determine the birth of a work that has gestated but has not found the right portal for arrival.

A particular form has always appealed to me: separate, interlocking stories or vignettes that fit together like links of a necklace. Bite-sized, they're a pleasure to read, with their cord of continuity and tidy, self-contained structure. They usually stand on their own but have a cast of returning characters and a cumulative effect when read together. It is the form of *Winesburg, Ohio*, *The Joy Luck Club*, and Alice Munro's early story collections.

This is a less daunting form to contemplate than a novel, especially in the beginning, and can be used effectively in both fiction and nonfiction.

Whatever your taste, saturate yourself in the form that appeals to you.

Read what you're pining to write.

Some writers worry that they'll be swayed if they read other people's work. But as Virginia Woolf once said, books are extensions of each other, despite our tendency to view them separately.

In the end, all of us are submerged in the same pool of words.

Pick an episode from your turning points, and write about it as journalistically as possible, describing it as if there were a video camera in the room. If you're writing about the day you lost your virginity, for example, describe the room you were in, the view from the window, the clothes you were wearing, your lover's face, any words of dialogue you can remember, how you felt inside your body.

Now take this same episode and allow yourself to wander away from the truth. Fictionalize as many components as possible. Make your lover more or less desirable, the outcome better or worse. Imagine the episode culminating in epiphany or disaster. Conjure up new dialogue or a different outcome, perhaps what could have—or should have—happened.

CHAPTER 10

ANGLE OF APPROACH

There is not one of us who could not also be someone else. A shrub is content for the time being to remain one. But people can, so to speak, become anything, incomplete as they are. Dark and indefinite as they are in themselves, in their folds.

—ERNEST BLOCK

Thirty years ago my older brother, who was ten years old at the time, was trying to get a report on birds written that he'd had three months to write. It was due the next day. We were out at our family cabin in Bolinas, and he was at the kitchen table close to tears, surrounded by binder paper and pencils and unopened books on birds, immobilized by the hugeness of the task ahead. Then my father sat down beside him, put his arm around my brother's shoulder and said, "Bird by bird, buddy. Just take it bird by bird."

—ANNE LAMOTT

Like most everyone else, when I first started writing I only used the first person.

There was no other choice. I was so self-absorbed, such a swollen presence, that my persona took up the whole horizon, blotting out the light of any other point of view.

This made it easy to cast myself in heroic lights in my autobiographical fiction, especially my exile to a home for unwed mothers, where I often starred myself, banished and bloated, forced to recite Bible verses before supper and mop the floor on my hands and knees.

That the father of my child was African-American made my urge for self-aggrandizement even more irresistible. I could steer right into the well-worn track of a hundred other blighted love stories, make the two of us star-crossed lovers, stymied by the world.

No matter that I had sought him out in the first place to make another boy jealous or that he had originally been more interested in my friend than in me. What kind of story was that? First-person narration could transport me away from the drabness of the truth.

So while it was perfectly true that the only verse I ever recited at dinnertime was "Jesus Wept," that I rebuffed the

bouffant-haired evangelical housewives who tried to save
me and refused the Gideon the headmistress stuffed in my
lap on my way to the hospital, in my plumped-up first person, I spit the verses, railed at the housewives, hurled the
Bible with a flair and fervor I never managed in real life.

And who did I do this for?

Myself. No one was reading what I wrote, and I had no
reason to believe they ever would. Part of my need to write
this way was in revolt against the mute anonymity I was
meant to maintain.

This was the Midwest Way: to endure in silence, then
keep moving, stepping over the pain.

I could almost do this, but not completely, and so writing allowed me to discharge certain feelings that had
nowhere else to go—not wanting to complain to my family and believing that I deserved certain punishment for
being caught as well as bad.

Nor could I talk to the so-called birth father, who by
then was heading to Vietnam. The only photo I'd spirited
away with me was a Polaroid of him posing, playboy-like,
in an all-white jumpsuit. It was easier to smear him into
my tableau of injustice when I left his photo hidden in my
nightstand.

Over the years, I continued to star myself in these triumphant first-person narratives, just as I continued to gild

our old love affair. I did this for twenty-seven years until a day when I stood at the airport and watched the long legs of my daughter stride out of the middle distance. There was my whole wayward past, the sweet, ruddy Germans of my side converging with the long bones and deep tones of my boyfriend's line.

Over my years of conjuring my daughter, I had consulted Ouija boards and phoned detectives. In my writing, I'd named her Kay, Rita, and Carlotte; I'd given her auburn hair, umber skin, mossy eyes.

But my poor imagination had been unable to concoct such a clavicle or jawline; the white flash of teeth embedded like jewelry; the cut and drape of how she was knit together, the hosts I could see trailing behind her.

I dropped my pen at the flesh and blood of her.

In the face of this, who needed fiction anymore?

Whose Head, Whose Eyes?

Everything turns on point of view—on whose head you're in, whose eyes you're peering out from.

Compare Osama bin Laden's view of America with George W. Bush's; Monica Lewinsky's version of an hour in the White House—what she hoped for, what the interior voice in her head was saying—with the same scene from the point of view of Bill Clinton.

Point of view really means just this: who is observing the scene and where is she or he perched to do so?

Person, on the other hand, is the division that tells us who is speaking.

There is an intimacy to the first person, the voice that comes most easily to us, that we use in letters and journals, autobiography and memoir.

We might think of it simply as our own real voice without realizing how it can shift depending on the use we put it to, whether it's used in fiction or memoir.

But the first person can become as tedious as staring in a mirror. Switching to the third person can give you access to a whole new area of information. It can change your perspective entirely.

The third person involves climbing up the neck and into the head of the man sitting next to you on the bus, in his Sansabelt slacks and Dacron windbreaker, with his Hammond, Indiana, childhood and his psoriasis and his cravings for nuts and beer.

Climbing into another person like this can open up the book of the world.

Knowing Junior

What follows is part of a story I wrote about a character named Junior Johnson, a black mortician who takes revenge on a racist English teacher from his past by dissecting her brain.

In 1970, on the south side of Union, Ohio, Junior Johnson embalmed bodies, so he knew it was a lie about people being the same inside. In fact, everyone was different, even more different than you would think. Pretty women with unlined faces had brown clotted blood and mouths that fell open like doors when they died. Big men in pallid suits deflated like rag dolls when their spirits were gone—Junior had to stuff their small forms with rags; newspaper rustled too much. But it was the whites who were most frightening—across the board, whoever they were, they shrank up and took on the ice blue cast of ghosts when they passed on.

The evening of Mrs. Holmes's arrival, 37 Park Avenue held only two bodies, and one of them, Junior, couldn't settle down. He drank bourbon and water, he counted money, but none of his usual occupations helped. As if in a trance, he wandered down to the bookshelf in his study and pulled out his yellowed high school yearbook, which fell open to the faculty section. Junior only turned one page, and there she was: Mrs. James Holmes, a hundred years younger and with a different name, Miss Edith Hutt, Miami University, Bachelor of Arts. The same livery lips and mottled neck, even then. Now that he saw her, he remembered everything about the year when she'd taught him English; 1939 fanned out with facts. He had been the only black in the class excepting so-called retarded twins, Terry and Jerry Roberts, who stayed on for years after Junior graduated and were finally relegated to a semi-permanent state called special education. Junior had been eighteen and literature had excited him that year for the first and last time. But Miss Edith had taken care of that; she'd nipped that in the bud. He remembered her static notes on his theme books that he had covered with black ink from a fountain pen of his father's: "Stick to your topic! Don't ramble. What is your point?" Whatever Junior had to say about Shakespeare, about Chaucer, about Melville, it wasn't clear, it wasn't so, and it was usually too much. When he wrote "Ph.D." on a questionnaire she sent around asking for vocational plans, she had approached him with a bemused curl on her horrid lips and asked, "Ph.D. in what?"

Once I'd written this, I was reluctant to show it to anyone; even bypassing what such a story said about me, there

was this: what could I possibly know about a black mortician's life?

Not much, perhaps, but there were reasons I was driven
to try to imagine it.

Even as a child, I was preoccupied with death, having
been mightily affected by the few funeral homes I had visited—studying great-grandparents, waxen in caskets, still
wearing their spectacles.

I studied the life cycles of tadpoles and caterpillars in
our World Book, following the circular arrows that led to
frog, to monarch, then death. Was this it for us? Were we
also just *nature*? Would I simply grow higher and heavier—
no wings or stripes—only to simply die?

And if this was so, what was the point of all the rules?
Why couldn't I skip school and run about feral and naked,
peeing in leaves and eating candy until my teeth were rot-
ted stubs?

The way I saw it (and the way Junior Johnson later saw
it), instead of imbuing life with meaning, death made it all
seem a terrible waste.

And I knew about certain black men in the way you
know people from sitting at their tables and lounging
among their fathers and uncles as they watch NCAA
championships on Sunday afternoons, drinking beer.

And finally, notably, I'd suffered in high school under a

liver-lipped, bilious teacher, who was a member of the John Birch Society, and from whose teeth dripped a rancid racial hate.

All these various tendencies and preoccupations were eventually swept into a corner to form this story of Junior.

Experiment

If you find yourself telling the same story over and over, but in a way you don't find satisfying, try changing person or point of view.

You can use disguise as a way of critically distancing yourself from a story you may be too close to.

You can experiment with an unreliable narrator, as Eudora Welty does in her story "Why I Live at the P.O." From the first paragraph, we sense that the person speaking is not entirely to be trusted.

I was getting along fine with Mama, Papa-Daddy and Uncle Rondo until my sister Stella-Rondo just separated from her husband and came back home again. Mr. Whitaker! Of course I went with Mr. Whitaker first, when he first appeared here in China Grove, taking "Pose Yourself" photos, and Stella-Rondo broke us up. Told him I was one-sided. Bigger on one side than the other, which is a deliberate, calculated falsehood: I'm the same.

You can employ the rarely used second person, as Joan Chase does in *During the Reign of the Queen of Persia:*

We four climb up into the haymow, up to the rafter window. We vow we will never forgive him. We swear to avenge ourselves, even if we have to pay with our lives. We tell each other how he'd feel if we died.

You can enter the consciousness of a house, as Toni Morrison does in *Beloved:*

124 was spiteful, full of a baby's venom. The women in the house knew it and so did the children.

Or personify a city, as E. M. Forster does in *Howards End:*

London was beginning to illuminate herself against the night. Electric lights sizzled and jagged in the main thoroughfares, gas lamps in the side-streets glimmered a canary gold or green. The sky was a crimson battlefield of spring, but London was not afraid.

Or try something really challenging—write from the point of view of one of your parents.

Carolyn Heilbrun has said there is no woman who feels her mother loved her enough. And this is perhaps also true with fathers and sons.

Because of the prism of love and ambivalence through which most of us view our parents, writing from their point of view can be a revealing exercise.

Mothers, in particular, are often our closest yet most mysterious figures, so near to us as to be rendered almost invisible. Trying to write from a mother's consciousness can be deeply illuminating.

Amy Tan, in writing her mother's obituary, says:

. . . I realized there was still much that I did not know about my mother. Though I had written three novels informed by her life, she remained a source of revelation and surprise.

In *Amy and Isabelle*, Elizabeth Strout manages the remarkable—inhabiting the minds of *both* mother and daughter, using an omniscient point of view.

Isabelle (Mother)
In all the times Isabelle had imagined Amy on some college campus, she had never imagined what she saw

now: her daughter would be ashamed of her. Amy, walking across a leafy lawn, laughing with her new, intelligent friends, was not going to say My mother works in a mill. She was not going to invite these girls home on weekends or holidays, and neither would she share with Isabelle the wonderful things she was learning, because in her eyes Isabelle was a small-town dummy who worked in a mill.

Amy (Daughter)

The real problem, of course, was that Amy and her mother were together all day. To Amy it seemed as though a black line connected them, nothing bigger than something drawn with a pencil, perhaps, but a line that was always there. Even if one of them left the room, went to the ladies' room or to the water fountain out in the hall, let's say, it didn't matter to the black line; it simply cut through the wall and connected them still.

For my part, I remember a moment when I awoke—if only briefly—to my mother's consciousness, approaching her as she waited for me on a corner during a trip we took together to Paris, seeing her with a sudden flash of clarity as *another woman.*

Maybe it was being in a foreign place where we'd both reverted to bumbling midwesterners, dropping francs down storm sewers and fracturing words with our literal tongues.

But for whatever reason, the obliterating shell of her motherhood cracked for me that day—or maybe it was the crust of my daughterly self-absorption. All at once I could feel what it must have been like to be her, looking down the rue du Rivoli for a daughter who'd had to wade into middle age before she was able to see her.

In spite of this, I have never been able to write from my mother's point of view.

And I have never entirely escaped the first person, but I've learned something vital about it over the years.

"I" is a character with all the foibles and flaws of any other.

You may write as if your "I" knows everything, but she doesn't, and neither do you.

Pick a traumatic event from your past that involves another person—the day your friend betrayed you, your lover cheated on you, your father deserted your family. Write about it in the first person, telling about it as if you were talking to a friend or confiding it in a diary.

Now make the monumental shift and write the same episode using the other person's point of view—the friend, lover, or father. Allow your writing to adapt and flow with the adjustments this shift creates.

Try to imagine the other person's motivation and inner dialogue.

What was your friend thinking when she lied to you?

What was your father's motivation when he left your family for another life?

How did your lover feel when he told you he was leaving you for someone else? How did he see you? What were his inner thoughts?

Allow yourself to be seen as a character through the other person's eyes.

EDITING—AT LAST

Old paint on canvas as it ages sometimes becomes transparent. When that happens it is possible, in some pictures, to see the original lines: a tree will show through a lady's dress, a child makes way for a dog, a large boat is no longer on an open sea. That is called pentimento, because the painter has repented, changed her mind. Perhaps it would be as well to say that old conceptions, replaced by a latter choice, is a way of seeing and then seeing again.

—LILLIAN HELLMAN

Muddiness is not merely a disturber of prose, it is a destroyer of life, of hope: death on the highway caused by a badly worded road sign, heart-break among lovers caused by a misplaced phrase in a well-intentioned letter, anguish of a traveler expecting to be met at the railroad station and not being met because of a slipshod telegram.

—WILLIAM STRUNK JR.

When I was a girl I had fantasies that now seem pathetic—one was to be let loose in a grocery with endless funds and no one to monitor me, free to pursue my own personal food pyramid—heavy on nuts and caramel and topped by a heavy tier of cheese.

A later dream was to break free of the restraints of post-adolescence, the brassiere straps and curfews, the tucked waists and menstrual laws, so that I could slump, jump, and generally make a mess, *be* a mess again.

Writing incorporates both these dreams—I can take anything I want from my memory's store without cost or permission and make a mess with it, writing on the back of electric bills and napkins, following any thought I please. I can write as long as I want, say as much as I can, and relish the words revealing what I really think, like magic ink rising up with a message.

No one can stop me. And I can do this in the middle of the night in ratty robes and unkempt hair, in the midst of ringing phones and unpaid bills.

But after all this, then what?

It depends.

There doesn't have to *be* a next, for one thing. To insist that writing always has to become something is like barging into someone's shower while she's singing and asking: "What are you planning to do with that song?"

There is no reason why you shouldn't continue writing in this way for your own self-discovery and pleasure. This is the nature of journal and diary writing, an unending stream of writing that is meant for your own enlightenment and surprise.

But if you reach a point where you want to develop and structure what you've written in order to submit or refine it, then it's time for the dire character we've kept in the closet until now—the editor, in her glen plaid skirt and dangling reading glasses, sitting behind a desk with her primers and sharpened pencils. The editor is not someone you want to fraternize with regularly; she is cutthroat and without mercy. The eye of the world is embedded in her.

In my case, she is Miss C, my scathing, hawkeyed high school business teacher, queen of the timed typing test, rapper of the pica-elite ruler, who claimed to be able to tell who wasn't a virgin simply by looking her in the eye.

She was the slashing red-penned corrector of my past, who had no stomach for messes, excess, or emotion, and was on the lookout for the point, the big point, of anything ever written.

Why would we invite someone like her in at all, even for a moment?

Because just as we occasionally need periodontists and other painful professionals, we have brief need for her now. Her very ruthlessness can be useful: with her disdain for flab and excess, she is the one who can tell you what must go.

As you let her in, make sure you're not also allowing in the Angel in the House or one of her minions. Don't let any of them elbow their way in with their critical whispers and ego-driven fears.

Just let in your dispassionate, clear-eyed editor.

Give her a hard-backed chair and a glass of water.

Shut off the rest of the house and turn over the hourglass.

Let her know you're limiting her venue and time.

Seeing Again

Editing is located on the other side of the room, the other side of the fence, the other side of the brain from writing. It is in direct opposition, even competition, with writing. As in Lillian Hellman's pentimento, it is the time for seeing your work again.

Editing involves external and internal insight; you have to view your writing with a fresh eye in order to shape and revise it. Peter Elbow compares it to being a sculptor, peeling off layers of stone to reveal the figure beneath.

It can involve pruning and deadheading or major transplantation, moving the apple tree you were so sure would be the center of your front yard to the corner of the back where it can get the sun it needs.

It's the time to finally ask the questions:

What do I really mean to say?

How can I make it unified and clear?

Tell your editor to look for:

FANCY OVERWROUGHTNESS

He peered at her with pellucid gray eyes and opined sexily, "You're beauteous."

AND MAKE IT NATURAL

He turned his gaze on her and said, "You're great."

PASSIVE DRABNESS

A good time was had by all.

AND TURN IT TO ACTIVE CLARITY

The girl's basketball team ate spaghetti marinara and told rude jokes about their coach on Tuesday night at Sagglio's Pizzeria.

DEADWOOD

It was a rather little boat that was very pretty.

AND BE CONCISE

It was a trim, appealing skiff.

CLICHÉS

When they made love, flames of desire leapt through her body as they soared to new heights.

AND SAY IT YOUR OWN WAY

He led her into the dark and knew what to do with her, without fumblings or apology.

This is also the time in the writing process to:

Be specific
Move sections
Approach from another angle
Change point of view or person
Listen to the reactions of readers

And remember what Grace Paley said: "If you say what's on your mind in the language that comes from your parents and your streets and friends, you'll probably say something beautiful."

One student used the following method, especially when she was in a crunch, to compress the whole process we've been exploring.

It's too concentrated a method for my taste, especially for the relaxed, exploratory writing we're doing. But spread out over months, it's a nice plan.

1. Write automatically for an hour without any inhibitions: no rereading, editing, or trying to be good. When you're finished, highlight your strongest points.
2. Beginning with these points, write exactly as you did the first hour, then highlight your strongest points again.
3. Now that you know what you're driving at, identify your best points, edit, organize, and structure.

Recasting

In the editing process, there are times when nothing less than a rewrite will do. Surface repair is just not adequate when there are deep fissures, internal weaknesses that threaten the inner stability of your work.

In this case, you need someone brawnier than your pleated-skirted editor; you need a heavy lifter, with a spade and shovels and an iron disposition. You need someone strong enough to heave over an old stale section to see what is lurking underneath.

Recasting requires patience and time and re-envisioning. You can't rush it. In speaking of the ten years she spent writing her second novel, Donna Tartt says, "Writing over a long period of time, one builds up a sense of richness and verisimilitude that is impossible to fake."

If you continue to feel stymied about a piece of writing and all else fails, place it in a drawer and see what occurs to you when you are not consciously laboring to fix it. Take a walk, swim, move your body—the rhythm of repetitive movement can call forth words and bring thoughts into focus.

The breakthrough of ideas from below the level of awareness often occurs when you have stopped trying to figure things out. Einstein likened the generation of a new idea to a chicken's laying an egg: *Kieks—auf einmal ist es da.* Cheep—and all at once, there it is. You need to change the point of view, you need to dramatize; you really want to write a story, not a poem.

Carson McCullers says:

The dimensions of a work of art are seldom realized by the author until the work is accomplished. It is like a flowering dream. Ideas grow, budding silently, and there are a thousand illuminations coming day by day as the work progresses. A seed grows in writing as in nature. The seed of the idea is developed by both labor and the unconscious and the struggle that goes on between them.

If a piece has no energy, be brave, face facts. You can prop it up, dress it up in borrowed finery, but it probably won't help. Step over it and move on. There is more to write, always, and nothing is wasted.

Get Her Out

The problem with the editor is that once you let her in, she may take off her shoes, curl up on the couch, and want to stay a while. She may start making comments that far exceed her purview.

She may start advising you on what topics to write about or challenge your need to write at all.

So it's important to kick her out as soon as her work is finished.

Then, as soon as she's gone, invite your wild self back in. She's the one who will be your producer. She's the one who knows that your words need to go through different stages without taking shortcuts.

She's your real writing companion, the one who holds the key to your door.

Reread what you've written in the last weeks.

What does it say to you?

What themes and preoccupations keep reappearing?

What images recur?

Do you feel drawn to a particular point of view or form?

With a marker, underline passages in your writing that seem alive and strong to you. Is there more you could explore here? Could you continue writing from any of these sections?

Underline in another color the parts of your writing that feel weak or cool. Look at these cool parts again. Turn them over.

What's underneath these sections that is truer? Approach them again and see if you can dig deeper.

NINE GOOD THINGS ABOUT WRITING

There is a vitality, a life force, an energy, a quickening that is translated through you into action, and because there is only one of you in all of time, this expression is unique. And if you block it, it will never exist through any other medium and be lost. It is not your business to determine how good it is, nor how valuable, nor how it compares with other expressions. It is your business to keep it yours, clearly and directly to keep the channel open. You do not even have to believe in yourself or your work. You have to keep open and aware to the urges that motivate you. Keep the channel open.

—MARTHA GRAHAM

Talent is nothing but long patience.

—FLAUBERT

The hard truths of writing are the ones you always hear about—the terror of the blank page, the loneliness, the writing blocks.

The way everyone in the world seems to be writing and no one in the world seems to be reading.

The death of the poem, the novel, of literacy itself.

Yet there are also positive things to say about writing, especially personal writing, which is the freest of all.

1. THEY CAN'T TAKE THAT AWAY FROM YOU

Your story is yours—it's probably the only thing that *is* all yours—and you have the right to twist and turn and record it in any form you wish, whether in a journal, as memoir, fiction, or poetry.

Writing requires no degree or connections; no thesis adviser or special skills, no permission from anyone but yourself.

There's no other artistic endeavor so democratic, so open to all, as writing.

The common language of ordinary life is beautiful. If you've lived, you have a story, pure and simple, and it's as worthy as anyone's.

2. NO HANDICAP CAN STOP YOU

The urge to communicate what we know and who we are is powerful enough to overpower most any handicap or obstacle.

In my circle of acquaintances, I've known a woman with Lou Gehrig's disease, a young man who became para-plegic after a motorcycle accident, and a woman who was confined to bed with back injuries who all found writing a release and great solace.

One workshop participant was manic-depressive, a detail he reported as matter-of-factly as his name. But there was no need for him to tell us which state he was in at the start of each session; I could tell by what he wrote. When he was in manic mode, his poetry was all over the blackboard—tiny words, wild and spidery, spiraling in designs.

In his depressive mode, however, his poetry was com-pletely different. On the page, for one thing, and more dense, compact, and haiku-like. It seemed to ease some-thing in him to emit his words in these differing ways depending upon his condition. He knew what he was doing; he knew how to help himself with writing. You could see it did him good.

3. SHARING HELPS

Once we all were linked by cautionary tales and purposeful stories, passed down to encourage or advise us. We heard about the field a great-grandfather broke his heart over, the man who lured an aunt across state lines. But many of us now live in the center of an opaque past, memories piled in dusty corners. There's no trail for us to follow and we're too harried to leave one ourselves.

Yet we still retain a primal urge for stories, the same way we hanker for sugar and salt; we yearn to sit down and be swept away by other people's tales; we ache to tell them ourselves.

Forming a group, online or in person, with like-minded writers and readers, can be a boon to a regular writing regimen as well as providing a place to share work. Reading your own work aloud can be an affirming experience that enhances your sense of accomplishment.

The challenge for the members of such groups is to have the bravery to be critical and the sensitivity to be constructive, to be, as Philip Larkin said, "both not untrue and not unkind."

Online classes are an option. I was skeptical of cyberclasses until I led one. Nowhere else is the sheer power of words more evident than in these kind of groups, where you are free from the mighty distractions of bodies, with their deodorants and hairstyles, their vexing odors and shapes. In an online class, you are pure words—a name to begin with, then whatever syllables you send out over the ether. You can mix together people and perspectives as far-flung as Alaska and Athens. And unlike other groups, which may veer off into socializing, words are more likely to remain the central focus.

Because of this, people in online groups may end up paradoxically feeling closer than participants in other settings, where the vexing shadow of the corporeal self tends to distract and waylay.

It's not that egos don't burn through cyberspace, they do, but they're unconnected with the body. Your good looks—or lack of them—don't count online. Indeed I've had students who enroll in online classes expressly because there is some issue or trouble about their body. In this way, sharing online bypasses some of the more peevish distractions of literal groups.

If you can't find a group and yearn to be read, establish a reading relationship with someone you trust, a reciprocal one if possible. But be cautious about handing over your writing to those you're close to if you're expecting them to love it—or you, for writing.

4. THERE'S ALWAYS MORE

Just when you think you have nothing further to say, you probably do.

Avoid the tendency to stop writing too early. There's an artificial wall, a stopping place, in many of us that needs to be pushed through. It often occurs right before a breakthrough, just ahead of a realization.

The next time you feel you have finished writing, get up and look out the window, take a walk, but don't close your notebook just yet. Give yourself that afterperiod to see what arises. Then go back to your desk, draw a line under your last sentence, and continue. You may be surprised at what comes next.

Or put it away and take it out the next day, when you're feeling fresh. For many of us, the best time to work is first thing in the morning, when we're closest to the unconscious, as opposed to the riddled hyperconsciousness of evening, when we're buried under the accumulated debris of the end of the day. The morning is different—ushered out of the netherworld of dreams, we are still connected to something larger than ourselves.

5. YOU CAN ALWAYS BECOME UNSTUCK

Edna O'Brien says:

> When a writer or an artist has the feeling that he can't do it anymore, he descends into hell. So you must keep in mind that although it may stop, it can come back. When I was a child in Ireland, a spring would suddenly appear and yield forth buckets of beautiful clear water, then just as suddenly it would dry up. The water diviners would come with their rods and sometimes another spring would be found. One has to be one's own water diviner.

So how do you become your own water diviner?

- Pay attention to what comes to you unbidden—a thought in the middle of the night, a notion that won't go away. Write it down or it will slip away.
- Write in small scenes or episodes. Stop the video in your mind on a particular frame and write about it, being as specific as possible.
- Allow one remembrance to trigger another.
- Look at old photos and letters; talk to family members and friends about the past.
- Try writing a letter to:

a daughter, telling a story from your childhood

an old lover, telling him or her what you really meant
to say

a dead relative, confessing something

a best friend, confiding a secret

- And if all else fails, ask yourself:

Is there something I'm avoiding?

Is the Angel in the House lurking behind the curtain,
or has the editor barged in before her time?

Do I really want to be writing this? If not, don't. Life is
too short. Writing should not be drudgery or duty
but pleasure.

6. YOU CAN PUBLISH YOURSELF

People are in such a rush to be "good" or published before
undertaking a regular, exploratory writing routine that is
rooted in experimentation and a sense of adventure. Give
yourself at least a year or two when you expect nothing of
yourself except to write regularly.

However, if you find yourself ready for publishing, you
might consider the many avenues for self-publishing,
which have democratized publishing, transforming writers
into authors for a relatively small fee.

Xlibris, summarized below, is one of several.

You upload your manuscript; they process it, format it, design the cover, assign it an ISBN, and register it as a trade paperback publication with Amazon, Borders, Barnes & Noble, and other bookselling channels. Your book is available from any retailer and from the Xlibris web site to any reader who orders it—printed on demand. You earn a fair royalty on every sale.

Plus you always control the rights to your book.

7. READING HELPS

Reading may be the best way—perhaps the *only* way—to learn anything worthwhile about the craft of writing. Only by reading do you absorb the architecture of form, the rhythm of dialogue, the feel of scene making; these skills grow in you as you read.

And there are certain writers whose work is so frank and alive that the act of reading them can, by association, encourage you to open yourself.

Here are a few who've done that for me:

Alice Munro, *The Moons of Jupiter* and *Friend of My Youth*
Lorrie Moore, *Birds of America*
Donna Tartt, *The Little Friend*
Michael Cunningham, *The Hours*

Jamaica Kincaid, *Annie John*

Elizabeth Strout, *Amy and Isabelle*

Toni Cade Bambara, *Gorilla, My Love*

Carson McCullers, *The Member of the Wedding*

Flannery O'Connor, *Selected Stories*

Toni Morrison, *Song of Solomon* and *Beloved*

Eudora Welty, *One Writer's Beginnings*

William Maxwell, *Billie Dyer and Other Stories, So Long, See
    You Tomorrow,* and *They Came Like Swallows*

Anne Tyler, *Saint Maybe*

Carolyn Heilbrun, *Writing a Woman's Life*

Dawn Powell, *My Home Is Far Away*

Rainer Maria Rilke, *Duinesian Elegies*

Nuala O'Faolain, *Are You Somebody?*

8. OLDER CAN BE BETTER

An old proverb says that every time an old man or woman dies, a library burns to the ground.

Writing is one of those artistic endeavors where age can be a bonus rather than a detriment. The older we are, the more material we have, the wiser we are, the wider our perspective.

The view at fifty is nothing like the view at thirty; seventy is nothing like twenty-two. When we're young we fill up the canvas; there is no foreground or background. But with time and trouble the aperture of the world opens wider; wisdom adheres to us like pollen.

We can't help but apprehend more, even if it seems no use to us. Even if we keep falling in the same ditches and breaking in the same places, at least we are aware of how many others are also lying there, before us and to come.

There are inner vistas and reservoirs of feeling that cannot be reached until time has passed, until you've felt your own body deepen, until you've left the mirror and opened your heart's door.

9. WRITING FEELS GOOD

It is satisfying to stimulate the part of the brain that
    remembers,
It's a pleasure to discern the geography of your own life,
Its shapeliness and architecture,
Its corners and blind alleys,
Where this veered off, and joined that,
To glimpse the intricate lacework of destiny and fate,
Of willfulness and luck, with its blind white face.

To see how a note sounded in youth tolls again later,
How one small turn leads to an unexpected landscape,

Windmills and poppies, a glimpse of the sea,
Writing like this, for self-revelation and discovery,
Is a quenching pleasure,
Like sipping water from a deep, cool well.

When I sat down years ago and began putting my story on paper, I was proclaiming something I didn't even believe—that my experience mattered.

Yours does, too.

Barry Lopez said, "Sometimes a person needs a story more than food to stay alive."

And I would add that sometimes a person also needs to write one.

BIBLIOGRAPHY

Akhmatova, Anna. *The Complete Poems of Anna Akhmatova*. Translated by Judith Hemschemeyer. Boston: Zephyr Press, 1983.

Anderson, Sherwood. *Winesburg, Ohio*. New York: Viking Press, 1960.

Angelou, Maya. *I Know Why the Caged Bird Sings*. New York: Bantam Books, 1983.

Bambara, Toni Cade. *Gorilla, My Love*. New York: Vintage Contemporaries, 1992.

Chase, Joan. *During the Reign of the Queen of Persia*. New York: Harper & Row, 1983.

Cunningham, Michael. *The Hours*. New York: Picador, 2002.

Elbow, Peter. *Writing Without Teachers*. New York: Oxford University Press, 1973.

English, Margaret. *The Brick House*. Xlibris, 2003.

Eugenides, Jeffrey. *Middlesex*. New York: Farrar, Straus & Giroux, 2002.

Forster, E. M. *Howards End*. New York: Penguin USA, 2000.

Frankl, Victor. *Man's Search for Meaning*. New York: Washington Square Press, 1998.

Garner, David. "Moore's Better Blues." Interview with Lorrie Moore. Salon.com, 1998.

Goldberg, Natalie. *Writing Down the Bones*. Boston: Shambhala Publications, 1986.

Hampl, Patricia. *I Could Tell You Stories*. New York: W. W. Norton, 1999.

Heard, Georgia. *Writing Toward Home*. Portsmouth, N.H.: Heinemann, 1995.

Heilbrun, Carolyn G. *Writing a Woman's Life*. New York: W. W. Norton, 1988.

Hellman, Lillian. *The Little Foxes*. In *Six Plays by Lillian Hellman*. New York: Vintage Books, 1979.

Johnson, Edgar. *Charles Dickens: His Tragedy and Triumph*. New York: Penguin Books, 1986.

Kincaid, Jamaica. *Annie John*. New York: New American Library, 1986.

———. *Lucy*. New York: Farrar, Straus & Giroux, 2002.

Krishnamurti, J. *Think on These Things*. Edited by D. Rajagopal. New York: HarperPerennial, 1989.

Lamott, Anne. *Bird by Bird: Some Instructions on Writing and Life*. New York: Doubleday, 1994.

Larson, Erik. *The Devil in the White City*. New York: Crown, 2003.

Lee, Harper. *To Kill a Mockingbird*. Philadelphia and New York: Lippincott, 1960.

Maxwell, William. *Billie Dyer and Other Stories*. New York: Random House, 1992.

———. *So Long, See You Tomorrow*. New York: Vintage, 1996.

———. *They Came Like Swallows*. New York: Vintage, 1997.

———. *Time Will Darken It*. New York, Vintage, 1997.

Maynard, Joyce. *At Home in the World*. New York: Picador, 1999.

McCullers, Carson. *The Member of the Wedding.* New York: Bantam, 1985.

Moore, Lorrie. *Birds of America.* New York: Knopf, 1998.

Moore, Thomas. *Care of the Soul: A Guide for Cultivating Depth and Sacredness in Everyday Life.* New York: HarperPerennial, 1994.

Morrison, Toni. *Beloved.* New York: Plume, 1998.

———. *Song of Solomon.* New York: Plume, 1987.

Munro, Alice. *Friend of My Youth.* New York: Random House, 1990.

———. *Lives of Girls and Women.* New York: Vintage, 2001.

———. *The Progress of Love.* New York: Vintage, 2000.

———. *The Moons of Jupiter.* New York: Vintage, 1994.

Nathan, Monique. *Virginia Woolf.* New York: Grove Press, 1961.

O'Connor, Sandra Day. *The Majesty of the Law: Reflections of a Supreme Court Justice.* New York: Random House, 2003.

O'Connor, Flannery. *Selected Stories.* New York: Farrar, Straus & Giroux, 1981.

O'Faolain, Nuala. *Are You Somebody?.* New York: Henry Holt, 1996.

Powell, Dawn. *My Home Is Far Away.* 1944. Reprint, South Royalton, Vt.: Steerforth Press, 1995.

Rilke, Maria Rainer. *Duinesian Elegies.* Translated by Elaine E. Boney. Chapel Hill: University of North Carolina Press, 1975.

Sanders, Lisa. "Diagnosis." *New York Times Magazine,* November 24, 2002.

Slater, Lauren. *Welcome to My Country: A Therapist's Memoir of Madness.* New York: Anchor, 1997.

Smyth, J. M.; Stone, A. A.; Hurewitz, A.; Kaell, A. "Effects of Writing about Stressful Experiences on Symptom Reduction in Patients with Asthma or Rheumatoid Arthritis: A Randomized Trial," *Journal of the American Medical Association* 281 (1999): 1304–9.

Spiegel, D. "Healing Words: Emotional Expression and Disease Outcome," *Journal of the American Medical Association* 281 (1999): 1328–29.

Sternberg, E. M. *The Balance Within: The Science Connecting Health and Emotions.* New York: W. H. Freeman, 2000.

Strout, Elizabeth. *Amy and Isabelle.* New York: Random House, 1998.

Styron, William. *Darkness Visible: A Memoir of Madness.* New York: Vintage, 1992.

Tan, Amy. *The Joy Luck Club.* New York: Putnam, 1989.

———. "Writers on Writing." *New York Times*, February 26, 2001.

Tartt, Donna. *The Little Friend.* New York: Knopf, 2002.

Taylor, Janelle. *Promise Me Forever.* New York: Kensington, 1992.

Tyler, Anne. *Saint Maybe.* New York: Ivy Books, 1998.

Van Devanter, Lynda, and Christopher Morgan. *Home Before Morning: The Story of an Army Nurse in Vietnam.* New York: Warner Books, 1990.

Welty, Eudora. "Why I Live at the P.O." In *The Collected Stories of Eudora Welty.* New York: Harcourt Brace Jovanovich, 1980.

Wharton, Edith. *The Age of Innocence.* New York: Modern Library, 1929.

———. *The House of Mirth.* New York: Signet Classic, 2000.

Woolf, Virginia. *A Room of One's Own.* New York: Harcourt Brace Jovanovich, 1929.

———. *A Writer's Diary.* New York: Harcourt Brace Jovanovich, 1953.

Zimmerman, Susan. *Writing to Heal the Soul.* New York: Three Rivers Press, 2002.

ABOUT THE AUTHOR

Lynn Lauber, fiction writer, essayist, and ghostwriter, has published two books of autobiographical fiction, *White Girls* (1990) and *21 Sugar Street* (1993), both published by W. W. Norton.

Her essays have appeared in the *New York Times* and anthologies such as *Wanting a Child* (Farrar, Straus & Giroux, 1999).

A longtime audiobook scriptwriter for Random House, she has also taught creative writing workshops around the country at colleges such as UCLA and Ohio State University, as well as at senior citizen centers, libraries, schools, and shelters. She lives in Nyack, New York. Her website address is www.LynnLauber.com.